W9-BJU-372

Kouts Public Library
101 E. Daumer Road
Kouts, IN 46347

Eyewitness
NORTH AMERICAN
INDIAN

Arapaho toy horse

Tlingit shaman's headdress

Dakota doll in traditional dress

Dakota pipe bag

North Greenland Inuit snow goggles

Dakota beaded vest

Choctaw sash

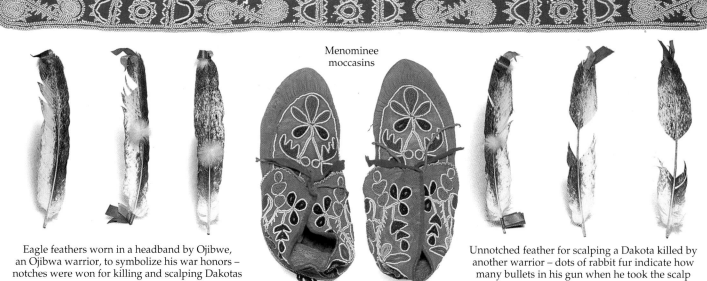

Menominee moccasins

Eagle feathers worn in a headband by Ojibwe, an Ojibwa warrior, to symbolize his war honors – notches were won for killing and scalping Dakotas

Unnotched feather for scalping a Dakota killed by another warrior – dots of rabbit fur indicate how many bullets in his gun when he took the scalp

Winnebago
roach
headdress

Tlingit hair
ornament made
from pig's tusk

Eyewitness
NORTH AMERICAN
INDIAN

Written by
DAVID MURDOCH

Chief Consultant
STANLEY A. FREED, PhD
Curator, Department of Anthropology, A.M.N.H.

Photographed by
LYNTON GARDINER

Pair of
Omaha
calumets

PORTER COUNTY PUBLIC LIBRARY

Kouts Public Library
101 E. Daumer Road
Kouts, IN 46347

DISCARD

J NF   970.00497 MUR   KO
Murdoch, David Hamilton, 1937-
North American Indian
33410009376965   APR 24 2008

Valparaiso - Porter County
Library System

DK

DK Publishing, Inc.
In association with
THE AMERICAN MUSEUM OF NATURAL HISTORY

Arapaho Ghost Dance club

Penobscot stone club

Dakota whistle

DK

LONDON, NEW YORK, MUNICH,
MELBOURNE, and DELHI

Project editor Marion Dent
Art editor Vicky Wharton
Managing editor Simon Adams
Managing art editor Julia Harris
Research Céline Carez
Picture research Sarah Moule
Production Catherine Semark
Editorial consultants Laila Williamson, Department
of Anthropology, and Scarlett Lovell, Director of Special
Publications, American Museum of Natural History, New
York; and Mary Ann Lynch

REVISED EDITION
Editors Elizabeth Hester, Laura Buller
Publishing director Beth Sutinis
Art director Dirk Kaufman
DTP designer Milos Orlovic
Production Chris Avgherinos, Ivor Parker

This Eyewitness ™ Book has been conceived by
Dorling Kindersley Limited and Editions Gallimard

This edition published in the United States in 2005
by DK Publishing, Inc.
375 Hudson Street, New York, NY 10014

07 08 09 10 9 8 7 6 5

Copyright © 1995, © 2005, Dorling Kindersley Limited

All rights reserved. No part of this publication may be
reproduced, stored in a retrieval system, or transmitted
in any form or by any means, electronic, mechanical,
photocopying, recording, or otherwise, without the
prior written permission of the copyright owner.
Published in Great Britain by Dorling Kindersley Limited.

Library of Congress Cataloging-in-Publication Data
Murdoch, David.
North American Indian/ written by David Murdoch
— 1st American ed.
p. cm. — (Eyewitness books)
1. Native American—Juvenile literature. [1. Native American]
I. Title.
CC171.M36 1995
930.1—dc20   94-9378
         ISBN-13: 978-0-7566-1082-1 (ALB)
         ISBN-13: 978-0-7566-1081-4 (PLC)

Color reproduction by
Colourscan, Singapore
Printed in China by Toppan Printing Co.,
(Shenzhen) Ltd

Discover more at
www.dk.com

Navajo quirt

Dakota war club

Apache war club

Apache tobacco pouch

Hopi bow and arrows

Contents

Blackfeet buffalo skull used in Sun Dance ceremony

Peopling of the Americas

WHO WERE THE FIRST AMERICANS? Archeologists agree that human beings probably trekked across the Ice Age land bridge from Siberia – but they do not agree on when this happened. Once thought to be 12,000 years ago, the date might be 40,000 years ago according to some new scientific theories. Some present-day Native North Americans believe their sacred stories place their beginnings in America, just as some Christians believe human beings were created in the Garden of Eden. Archeology shows that, however they got here, the first Americans, adapting to changing climate and environment, evolved from hunters using stone-tipped weapons to more advanced societies of farmers and artisans.

MIGRATION THEORY
During the Ice Age huge amounts of water froze into glaciers, Bering Strait became drained, and a wide, low, treeless plain (Beringia) connected Siberia and Alaska. About 12,000 years ago an ice-free corridor opened. Archeologists believe that paleo-Indians crossed Beringia, following the corridor to open country south of the glaciers.

Beringia

Ice-free corridor

Glacier (in violet)

Map of North America showing the human migration route from Siberia across the Ice Age land bridge

Exposed land (in green)

Model of an atlatl – from the Aztec word meaning "spear thrower"

Small Clovis point

Folsom point

Larger Clovis point could measure 5 in (13 cm) in length

Banner stone (a weight of stone) on which spear rested

ICE AGE HUNTERS
Definite proof of Ice Age human beings in America came in 1926, with the discovery at Folsom, New Mexico, of carefully shaped stone weapon points dating from 10,000 years ago. In 1932 weapon points from an even older people, up to 12,000 years ago, were unearthed at Clovis, New Mexico.

Wooden bar up to 3 ft (1 m) long

A STRONGER, LONGER THROW
Hunters of mammoths, mastodons, antique bison, and giant sloths from 10,000 years ago – such as the Folsom people in New Mexico – used an atlatl, a special device for throwing a spear. It was a bar with a flat stone on which the spear rested and a curved tip that engaged the spear's butt. The greater leverage gave a much stronger thrust.

Slate spear point from New England

Copper spear point from the Great Lakes area

Grip of hide with loops for fingers

Chipped-stone spear point from Tennessee

BECOMING EXTINCT
The end of the Ice Age, 10,000 years ago, saw many large animals, like the mammoth, become extinct, perhaps through environmental change or overhunting. From 5000 B.C. to 1000 B.C., the peoples of the Eastern forests learned to hunt woodland game. They lived in permanent settlements and developed complex societies. They were expert toolmakers, making a variety of spear points.

Copper spear point from the Great Lakes region

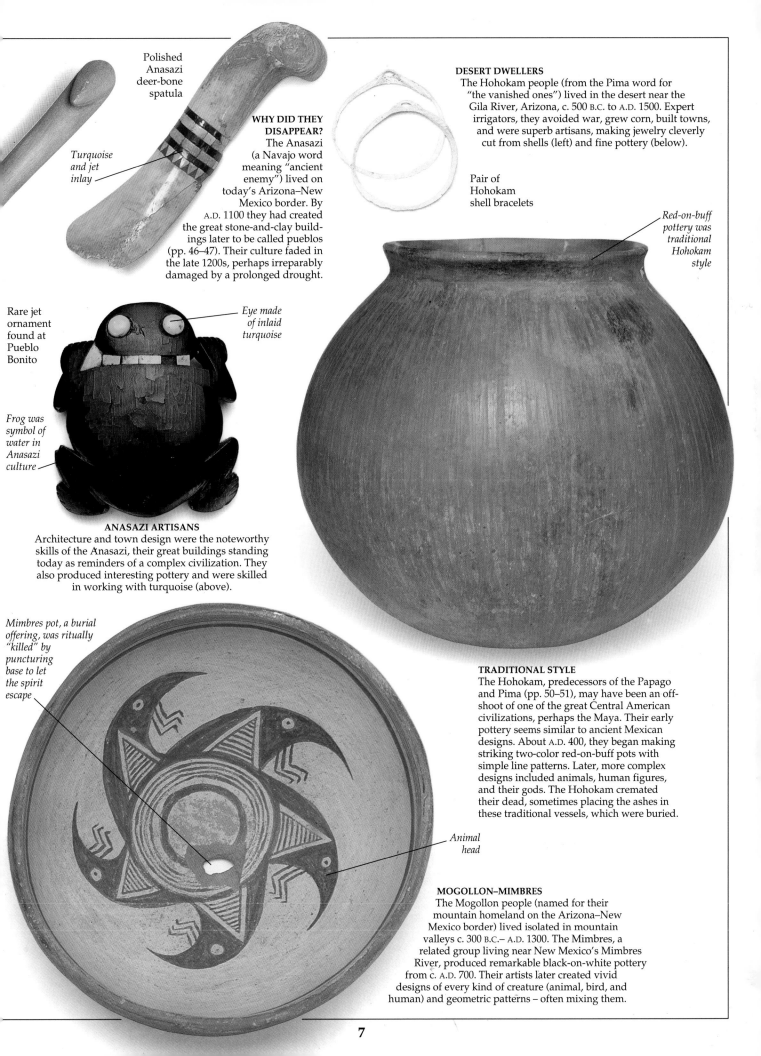

Polished
Anasazi
deer-bone
spatula

Turquoise and jet inlay

WHY DID THEY DISAPPEAR?
The Anasazi (a Navajo word meaning "ancient enemy") lived on today's Arizona–New Mexico border. By A.D. 1100 they had created the great stone-and-clay buildings later to be called pueblos (pp. 46–47). Their culture faded in the late 1200s, perhaps irreparably damaged by a prolonged drought.

DESERT DWELLERS
The Hohokam people (from the Pima word for "the vanished ones") lived in the desert near the Gila River, Arizona, c. 500 B.C. to A.D. 1500. Expert irrigators, they avoided war, grew corn, built towns, and were superb artisans, making jewelry cleverly cut from shells (left) and fine pottery (below).

Pair of
Hohokam
shell bracelets

Red-on-buff pottery was traditional Hohokam style

Rare jet ornament found at Pueblo Bonito

Eye made of inlaid turquoise

Frog was symbol of water in Anasazi culture

ANASAZI ARTISANS
Architecture and town design were the noteworthy skills of the Anasazi, their great buildings standing today as reminders of a complex civilization. They also produced interesting pottery and were skilled in working with turquoise (above).

Mimbres pot, a burial offering, was ritually "killed" by puncturing base to let the spirit escape

TRADITIONAL STYLE
The Hohokam, predecessors of the Papago and Pima (pp. 50–51), may have been an off-shoot of one of the great Central American civilizations, perhaps the Maya. Their early pottery seems similar to ancient Mexican designs. About A.D. 400, they began making striking two-color red-on-buff pots with simple line patterns. Later, more complex designs included animals, human figures, and their gods. The Hohokam cremated their dead, sometimes placing the ashes in these traditional vessels, which were buried.

Animal head

MOGOLLON–MIMBRES
The Mogollon people (named for their mountain homeland on the Arizona–New Mexico border) lived isolated in mountain valleys c. 300 B.C.– A.D. 1300. The Mimbres, a related group living near New Mexico's Mimbres River, produced remarkable black-on-white pottery from c. A.D. 700. Their artists later created vivid designs of every kind of creature (animal, bird, and human) and geometric patterns – often mixing them.

A vast continent

B<small>Y</small> 1500, T<small>HE</small> A<small>MERICAN</small> L<small>ANDS</small> north of Mexico were home to about 1.3 million people. Over 11,500 years, the descendants of the first Siberian migrants had diverged into more than 300 tribes – the densest population lived east of the Mississippi, in California, and in the Northwest. They had evolved ways of life exploiting food resources in different environments and developed high artistic skills. Their world was constantly changing – game animals became extinct; drought and tribal warfare led to migrations. Over the next 400 years, Europeans would bring about such catastrophic changes as loss of territory, population decline, and cultural restrictions for all Native North Americans.

Eagle feather tipped with horsehair

THE TERROR OF THE PLAINS
In 1500 the Cheyenne were not yet feared Plains warriors (pp. 28–29). Settled in villages in Minnesota, they farmed and hunted. They migrated westward in the mid-1700s, abandoning farming and becoming nomadic Plains horsemen dependent on the buffalo. An eagle-feather war bonnet (left) became their emblem of an experienced and respected warrior.

Red cloth, glass beads, and metal disk decorate headdress

Fur tassel

Ceremonial war bonnet of Cheyenne chief White Eagle

Apache buckskin cap decorated with glass beads and metal disk

Eagle-feather plumage

APACHE WARRIOR
The Apache (pp. 48–49) were newcomers in the Southwest in 1500; they seem to have migrated from Canada about 50 years earlier. The Spanish explorer Francisco de Coronado (1510–1554) thought the Chiricahua Apaches he met in 1540 were "a gentle people." Later Spaniards came to disagree with him!

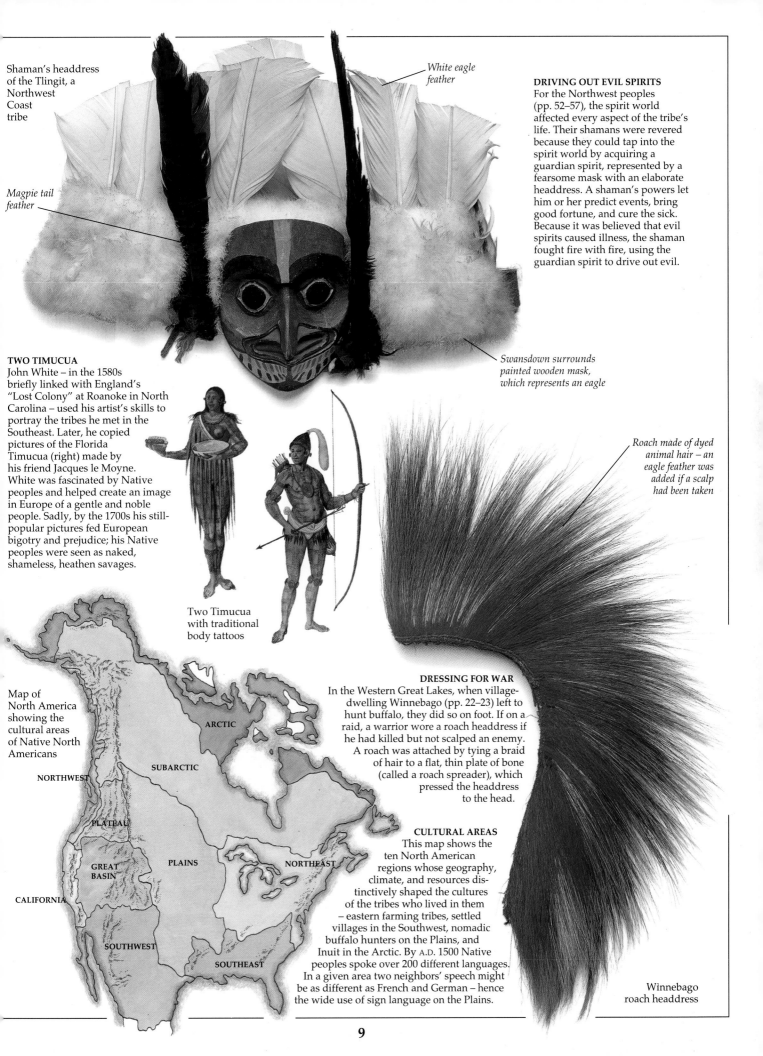

Shaman's headdress of the Tlingit, a Northwest Coast tribe

White eagle feather

Magpie tail feather

DRIVING OUT EVIL SPIRITS
For the Northwest peoples (pp. 52–57), the spirit world affected every aspect of the tribe's life. Their shamans were revered because they could tap into the spirit world by acquiring a guardian spirit, represented by a fearsome mask with an elaborate headdress. A shaman's powers let him or her predict events, bring good fortune, and cure the sick. Because it was believed that evil spirits caused illness, the shaman fought fire with fire, using the guardian spirit to drive out evil.

TWO TIMUCUA
John White – in the 1580s briefly linked with England's "Lost Colony" at Roanoke in North Carolina – used his artist's skills to portray the tribes he met in the Southeast. Later, he copied pictures of the Florida Timucua (right) made by his friend Jacques le Moyne. White was fascinated by Native peoples and helped create an image in Europe of a gentle and noble people. Sadly, by the 1700s his still-popular pictures fed European bigotry and prejudice; his Native peoples were seen as naked, shameless, heathen savages.

Swansdown surrounds painted wooden mask, which represents an eagle

Roach made of dyed animal hair – an eagle feather was added if a scalp had been taken

Two Timucua with traditional body tattoos

Map of North America showing the cultural areas of Native North Americans

ARCTIC

SUBARCTIC

NORTHWEST

PLATEAU

PLAINS

NORTHEAST

GREAT BASIN

CALIFORNIA

SOUTHWEST

SOUTHEAST

DRESSING FOR WAR
In the Western Great Lakes, when village-dwelling Winnebago (pp. 22–23) left to hunt buffalo, they did so on foot. If on a raid, a warrior wore a roach headdress if he had killed but not scalped an enemy. A roach was attached by tying a braid of hair to a flat, thin plate of bone (called a roach spreader), which pressed the headdress to the head.

CULTURAL AREAS
This map shows the ten North American regions whose geography, climate, and resources dis-tinctively shaped the cultures of the tribes who lived in them – eastern farming tribes, settled villages in the Southwest, nomadic buffalo hunters on the Plains, and Inuit in the Arctic. By A.D. 1500 Native peoples spoke over 200 different languages. In a given area two neighbors' speech might be as different as French and German – hence the wide use of sign language on the Plains.

Winnebago roach headdress

Medicine and the spirit world

POWER FILLED THE WORLD of the Native North American. Invisible but everywhere, this supernatural force of the spirit world touched people, animals, and plants. Shamans were special men and women who could heal the sick and capture some of this power to manipulate the ordinary world. Because shamans carried healing herbs, Europeans called them "medicine men," but for a shaman and the tribe all spirit power was "medicine." Shamans used dramatic ceremonies to help a patient's mind reject sickness. They also had drugs. The Five Tribes of the Southeast used the stimulant caffeine and salicylic acid (aspirin). Plains tribes used skunk-cabbage root for asthma and yarrow for minor wounds, both effective remedies. Shamans, like white doctors, were powerless against great European epidemics, especially smallpox which decimated the Native population, falling from 1.3 million people in 1500 to 400,000 before recovering.

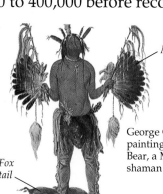

Medicine pipe

Fox tail

George Catlin painting of Old Bear, a Mandan shaman

OLD BEAR
The Mandan, like other Plains tribes, believed visions brought spirit-power. To receive a vision, a Mandan would seek solitude, pray, and abstain from food until near delirium. A truly powerful vision made its recipient a shaman. Dress and equipment (above) would be dictated by the shaman's first and later visions and would therefore contain power.

Tobacco bowl would be attached here

Sinew string

Animal and bird skins decorate this Blackfeet shaman's bearskin robe

A HEALING CEREMONY
American painter George Catlin (1796–1872) was determined to record the way of life of Native Americans before it was destroyed by whites. He made a tour of the American West (1830–36), having gained the confidence of 48 tribes, and produced over 500 vivid paintings and sketches and detailed notes. This portrait shows a Blackfeet shaman of the Plains performing a healing ceremony. Dressed in a bearskin robe, with the head forming a mask, the shaman danced around the patient.

Held by shaman during a healing ritual

Quinault carved wooden wand

HOW TO CURE A STOMACHACHE
The Hidatsa Plains tribe dealt with indigestion or other stomach pains by hand massaging or using a stomach pusher (above). With the patient laid flat, the curved end of this instrument (often made of white cedar) was rubbed against the stomach.

Double-mouthed sea lion's head

Elk bone

Abalone shell inlay

SHAMAN'S SPIRIT HELPER
Like all the tribes of the Northwest, the Quinault believed in a multitude of spirit beings who constantly affected the ordinary world. A shaman's powers came in part from his or her own special guardian spirit. As a doctor casting out an evil spirit, the shaman would carry a carving of the guardian spirit (above).

CATCHING A SOUL
Tsimshian shamans, like those of the other Northwest tribes, believed illness was caused either by an evil spirit or by the loss of the patient's soul – perhaps through a witch's spell. Therefore, one of the shaman's most important instruments was a soul catcher. A carved ivory or bone tube, it captured the soul and returned it to the body. Sometimes blowing through the soul catcher helped to expel the sickness.

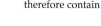

Copper wire wrapped tightly around pipe stem

Wooden pipe stem

Clutch of feathers dyed red

String of metal bells, which mimic sound of thunder during sacred ceremony

Beaded string attaches feather-and-animal-hair tassel to pipe

Animal fur decoration

FIRST SIGN OF THUNDER
Most revered of the Blackfeet sacred medicine pipes were the thunder pipes. At the first spring thunder, these pipes were removed from their bundles of sacred objects and offered to the thunder spirit. The ceremony asked protection from being struck by lightning (a frequent hazard on the Plains) and also for the power to heal sickness. Possessing a thunder pipe brought great prestige, but it was expected that ownership would be passed on to others.

Red, blue, yellow, and green geometric patterns were typical Dakota designs

Rawhide thong for tying lid

Side seam laced with red yarn over black fabric

Dakota medicine box and herbs

Eagle feather

Blackfeet sacred thunder medicine pipe

Roots wrapped in paper packet

A REMEDY FOR EVERYTHING
In addition to resorting to shamans, with their supernatural powers to cure illness, sick people had available various common medicines obtained from plants. This early 1900s Dakota medicine box contains herbs for headache, earache, stomach pain, bleeding, swelling, and other ailments. The selected herb was reduced to a powder on a tin grater and then steeped in hot water to make a healing tea.

Muslin packet containing herbs, tied with sinew

The far Northeast

A LAND OF ABUNDANT CONTRASTS, the wooded Northeast stretched from the St. Lawrence River to present-day North Carolina and west to the Mississippi. Its peoples made the most of an environment rich in game and fish. Except in the very cold far northern areas, they also raised corn, squash, and beans. Northern tribes, like the Penobscot and Malecite, living amid lakes and rivers, developed the birchbark canoe, much envied by their neighbors. From the early 1600s, fur trading with Europeans brought new materials and ideas. However, Northeast peoples (like the powerful Iroquois League) were drawn into the European struggle for North America in the 1700s and were forced to pick sides in the American Revolution (1775–1783) and the War of 1812. Most saw their independence destroyed and some were completely swept away by relentless American settlement.

INGENIOUS DESIGN
Tribes like Nova Scotia's Micmac exploited the fishing resources of their lakes and rivers, using hooks, lines, bows, traps, and spears. They liked to fish at night using birchbark torches. Attracted by the light, the fish came to the surface, where they were speared from birchbark canoes.

Wooden shaft of Micmac spear lashed to three barbs by cord

Central metal barb stabs fish

KING PHILIP
In 1675, angry and fearful at the growth of European power, "King Philip" (or Metacomet), chief of the Wampanoag, attacked the New England settlements. Eventually the rising was crushed, but if King Philip had formed more effective alliances with other tribes, the English colonies might have been destroyed.

Wooden side barb prevents fish from struggling free

Cord ties metal blade to wooden handle, providing a handy grip when drawn toward the woodworker

A CROOKED KNIFE
Birch bark was used to make canoes, wigwams, and paper. Bark sheets were cut with knives (like this Penobscot example). Holes were pierced along the edges with an awl and the sheets sewn together with spruce root to make storage or cooking vessels. Two-tone patterns were created by scraping away a dark coating on the bark's inner surface to reveal a lighter color.

Top (right) and side (below) views of model of a Malecite canoe

Low ends of canoe give it greater stability in calm waters; canoes with high bows and sterns provide protection from waves in choppy waters

Natural grain of bark, running longitudinally, allows sheets of bark to be sewn together more easily

Paddle up to 5 ft (1.5 m) long

Canoe up to 25 ft (7.5 m) long

Decorative shoulder fringing

Beaded flowers show European influence

EUROPEAN INFLUENCES
Before contact with Europeans, clothing in the Northeast was usually made from skins, sometimes decorated with painted symbols or dyed porcupine quills. European settlers brought new materials and decorations, such as woven cloth, glass beads, and tailored coats and trousers. The peoples of the Northeast adopted many of these innovations. Northeastern men traditionally wore a skin coat with painted decorations. This Penobscot buckskin jacket shows European influences – a tailored shape and elaborate glass-bead embroidery.

Stone club slotted into wooden handle

DEER SLAYER
Though the forest peoples were skilled at hunting, success was uncertain. Aid was sought from the spirit world through sacred charms and by rituals to contact the spirits of the slain animals. The chief hunting weapon was the bow and arrow, but a hit might not be fatal. A stone club (like this Penobscot example) was used for killing a wounded deer.

Struts made from split logs of white cedar

A DESIGN TRIUMPH
The best canoes were made from bark of the white birch, growing only in Canada and the most northeastern U.S. The framework was made of white cedar, split with hammers and wedges. It was covered with large sheets of bark laced together with roots and waterproofed with resin from the black spruce. Light enough to be carried, the canoe could take a load of 4,000 lb (1,800 kg). It was instantly adopted by European explorers and fur traders of the 1600s.

DECORATED DEERSKIN
Like all the peoples of the north-eastern forests, the Penobscot wore moccasins of deerskin, which were usually decorated. The influence of the Europeans shows in the lavish use of colored glass beads for decorations and the adoption of flower designs. Floral motifs were copied from white settlers and became widespread in the clothing of the Northeast. Men and women wore the same style of moccasin.

The League of the Iroquois

CORNPLANTER
Son of a Dutch trader father and a Seneca mother, Cornplanter (1740?–1836) fought Americans during the Revolution (1775–1783). Later this respected Seneca chief became a tireless spokesman for peace, negotiating many treaties.

Stone celt later replaced by steel blade

OUT OF THE NORTHERN WOODS early in the 1600s, there emerged the strongest political and military force in North America. Five tribes – the Mohawk, Onondaga, Seneca, Oneida, and Cayuga – ended their destructive feuding and formed the Iroquois League. Each tribe remained self-governing, but collective decisions were made by a representative Great Council. Though the members were men, they were chosen by the elder women of the tribes, who also had the power to remove them. The League was conceived to bring peace, but it became a formidable war machine. Because it was able to mobilize its forces effectively, it dominated much of the Northeast. Even as late as the mid-1700s it could hold the balance of power in the colonial wars between the French and the British.

TRIBES AT WAR
Iroquois wars were usually short raids with weapons like bows and war clubs. Involvement with Europeans competing with each other for the fur trade changed this. In 1649 the Iroquois League, as ally of the Dutch, virtually destroyed the Erie and Huron tribes, who supported the French.

Rattle made from a whole turtle shell

MOHAWK MUSIC
Music for the Mohawk, as for other eastern peoples, mostly depended on drums and rattles. A turtle-shell rattle was made by drying the animal, then cleaning out the shell, being careful to leave the head, tail, and legs intact. After this, pebbles were inserted and a wooden handle added.

HIAWATHA – A HERO
In the late 1500s, the prophet Dekana-widah, despairing at constant inter-tribal warfare, saw Iroquois union in a vision. Hiawatha, a Mohawk, then traveled ceaselessly between the tribes, persuading them to unite. *Hiawatha*, the famous poem by Henry Longfellow (1807–1882), gives no indication of the charisma and dip-lomatic skills of this remarkable leader.

Iroquois belts woven from wampum could be many feet long

Purple beads were twice as costly as white ones

THE COLOR PURPLE
Strings of purple and white tubular shell beads, called wampum, were used as symbolic gifts at marriages, as condolence to the bereaved, or as an invitation to ceremonies such as peace negotiations or a war alliance. White was the color of peace, black of gloomy matters. Purple was the most prized. Realizing the high value placed on it by the tribes, Europeans manufactured wampum from shell, using it in trade as money. Then they began to counterfeit it in glass. As money, wampum became debased and fell out of use.

Iroquois war club made in typical "rabbit's hind-leg" style

Elm-bark covering

Model of a four-fire, eight-family longhouse

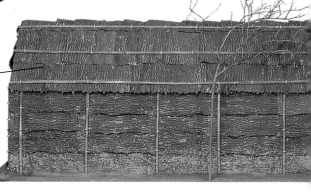

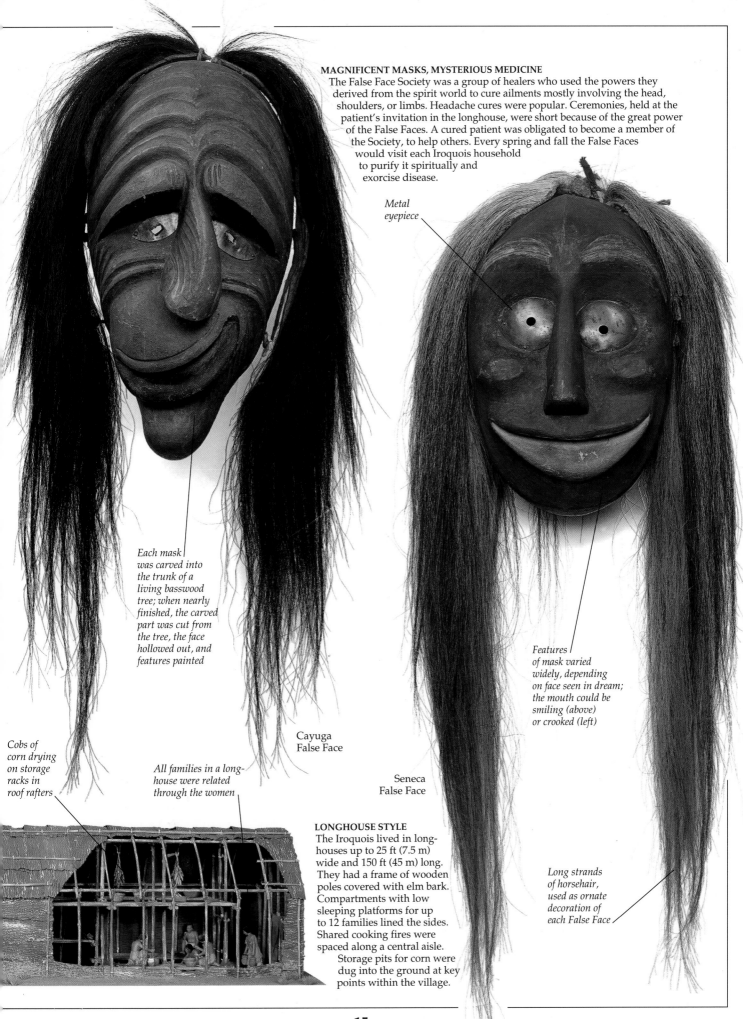

MAGNIFICENT MASKS, MYSTERIOUS MEDICINE
The False Face Society was a group of healers who used the powers they derived from the spirit world to cure ailments mostly involving the head, shoulders, or limbs. Headache cures were popular. Ceremonies, held at the patient's invitation in the longhouse, were short because of the great power of the False Faces. A cured patient was obligated to become a member of the Society, to help others. Every spring and fall the False Faces would visit each Iroquois household to purify it spiritually and exorcise disease.

Metal eyepiece

Each mask was carved into the trunk of a living basswood tree; when nearly finished, the carved part was cut from the tree, the face hollowed out, and features painted

Features of mask varied widely, depending on face seen in dream; the mouth could be smiling (above) or crooked (left)

Cayuga
False Face

Cobs of corn drying on storage racks in roof rafters

All families in a long-house were related through the women

Seneca
False Face

LONGHOUSE STYLE
The Iroquois lived in long-houses up to 25 ft (7.5 m) wide and 150 ft (45 m) long. They had a frame of wooden poles covered with elm bark. Compartments with low sleeping platforms for up to 12 families lined the sides. Shared cooking fires were spaced along a central aisle. Storage pits for corn were dug into the ground at key points within the village.

Long strands of horsehair, used as ornate decoration of each False Face

The three sisters

CORN WAS LIFE for tribes throughout the eastern woodlands. Producing starch to make energy, corn can provide 75 percent of the human body's food needs. Many corn varieties were grown (the Iroquois raised 15), and none required much labor. No care was necessary after planting the seed, except for scaring off birds, until the harvest. Beans and squash were often planted in the same field. Beans twined up the cornstalks, and squash choked weeds and kept the ground moist. The Iroquois believed these crops had spirit beings and called them "the three sisters." Dried and stored, corn, beans, and squash guaranteed food supplies, and more time could be devoted to ceremonies, hunting, trading, and war.

AUTUMN TREAT
Ripening in the autumn, pumpkin squash is a valuable vegetable. English colonists learned its use from Native Americans and invented sweet pumpkin pie, traditional at Thanksgiving.

Iroquois wooden bowl containing dried beans

BOWL OF BEANS
Depending on environment and accidents of history, many varieties of bean were grown across the continent. All had the same important qualities. They were a good extra food source because they had high amounts of proteins and essential vitamins (particularly of the Vitamin B group). Equally important, beans can be dried and stored for long periods, even years, without spoiling.

Ojibwa bark basket with dried rings of Sauk and Fox (Western Great Lakes tribes) squash plaited together

Seneca wooden pestle

Mohawk mortar made from hollowed-out tree trunk

DRIED SQUASH
Squashes grew thoughout the summer, when they were eaten fresh, providing an important source of Vitamin C, essential for general health. A portion of the crop was cut into strips or rings and sun-dried, or hung up whole inside the dwelling until dry, then stored with the beans and corn.

Iroquois harvesting basket containing cobs of Oneida dried corn

GRINDING CORN
Iroquois women shucked (stripped) the corncob of kernels with deer jawbones, then boiled the kernels in lye (made from boiled ashes) to soften the skins. Next the lye and skins were washed away in a special basket and the kernels were dried. They were turned into meal by laborious pounding with a mortar and pestle (left).

CORN ON THE COB
Some corn had to be saved for the lean winter months. Cobs were dried and hung in the longhouse. Some cobs were shucked and the kernels dried and stored in bins or underground granaries. Ground corn kernels were boiled as a porridge or made into cakes and eaten with maple sugar, honey, or fat.

MIDWINTER CEREMONIAL

The most solemn of the Iroquois ceremonies was held at midwinter, around the first of February. Messengers would stir the ashes of each longhouse fire, symbolizing the start of a new year. At the end of the four-day ceremony, the secret societies performed ritual dances. Among these was the Husk Face Society, whose members believed they were linked to spirit beings particularly connected with farming. Wearing sacred masks made from braided and sewn cornhusks, they danced to persuade the spirit world to ensure a good harvest and the birth of many children.

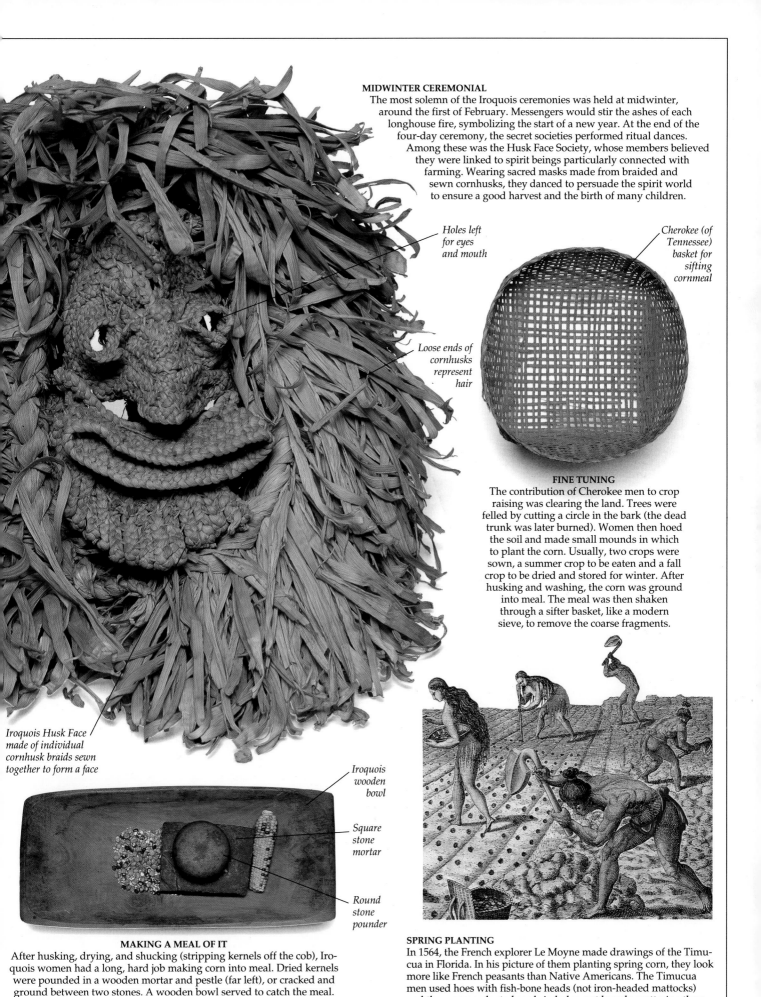

Holes left for eyes and mouth

Loose ends of cornhusks represent hair

Cherokee (of Tennessee) basket for sifting cornmeal

Iroquois Husk Face made of individual cornhusk braids sewn together to form a face

Iroquois wooden bowl

Square stone mortar

Round stone pounder

FINE TUNING
The contribution of Cherokee men to crop raising was clearing the land. Trees were felled by cutting a circle in the bark (the dead trunk was later burned). Women then hoed the soil and made small mounds in which to plant the corn. Usually, two crops were sown, a summer crop to be eaten and a fall crop to be dried and stored for winter. After husking and washing, the corn was ground into meal. The meal was then shaken through a sifter basket, like a modern sieve, to remove the coarse fragments.

MAKING A MEAL OF IT
After husking, drying, and shucking (stripping kernels off the cob), Iroquois women had a long, hard job making corn into meal. Dried kernels were pounded in a wooden mortar and pestle (far left), or cracked and ground between two stones. A wooden bowl served to catch the meal.

SPRING PLANTING
In 1564, the French explorer Le Moyne made drawings of the Timucua in Florida. In his picture of them planting spring corn, they look more like French peasants than Native Americans. The Timucua men used hoes with fish-bone heads (not iron-headed mattocks) and the women planted seeds in holes, not loosely scattering them.

The Mid-Atlantic Seaboard

A LAND OF WOODED PLAINS and lush valleys extended along the Mid-Atlantic Seaboard (Delaware, Maryland, Virginia, and North Carolina). Its people lived in villages of bark-covered, domed or arch-roofed dwellings. They raised corn and hunted in the forests. They were led by sachems (chiefs), who ruled by consensus. In 1585 John White, briefly part of the English colony at Roanoke (North Carolina) before it mysteriously disappeared, made paintings of the Secotan. Later published as engravings, they became the European stereotype of "Indians" for the next 200 years. When the English settled the colony of Virginia, they encountered the strong Powhatan alliance, which nearly destroyed them. Even more powerful were the Delaware, a confederation whose influence in the 1600s stretched far to the north and west. Their power was later broken by the Iroquois.

Delaware effigy of a woman, carved simply in wood

Elaborate decorations (silver crosses and buckles) show strong European influence

A SECOTAN VILLAGE
John White (pp. 8–9) painted this scene of a typical Secotan village in 1585. Shown are houses of bent saplings covered with bark and woven mats, surrounded by a defensive palisade (a circle of upright posts). The houses with sleeping platforms resemble those of the Iroquois to the north. The building with the cupola is a temple. Eventually the Secotan disappeared from their territory in North Carolina and were succeeded by other tribes.

A DOLL FOR HEALTH
The Delaware believed in the universal presence of the Great Spirit, and also in a world filled with lesser spirit beings. Spirits shaped their lives, fortunes, and health. Prayers, offerings, and ceremonies were meant to seek the help of these beings. This wooden image is a woman spirit guardian of health. Every fall the Delaware honored her with a feast, presents, and the sacrifice of a deer.

WOODLAND ART
With abundant forests, Eastern tribes used wood for many household utensils, such as bowls, spoons, and ladles. Woodworking was a task for men. To make hollow vessels like this bowl, the wood was first charred and the burned part scraped away with a stone (later iron) knife. Carved from the burled (knotty) parts of elm and maple, these objects were both useful and an expression of woodland art.

Handy hook topped with a crown

Simply carved wooden Delaware serving bowl and spoon

Paddle intricately carved with a star

Handle ornately carved with turtle, horse, and horseshoe

Delaware wooden food stirrer

Bottom filled with stones to sink basket to river bed

Delaware leggings made of woven cloth

WEARING APPAREL

Most clothing was made from animal skins, particularly deer hide. Men, taught from boyhood to ignore rain and chilly weather, wore only a breechcloth (front and back flaps held up by a belt) and moccasins in the warmer months, together with buckskin leggings. Women wore a waist-to-knee skirt over knee-high leggings. In winter both men and women added a fur robe. European contact brought woven cloth (left), which was sometimes substituted for skins, and new clothing patterns, such as jackets and trousers.

Decorated with deer-hoof rattles and silk ribbon appliqué

POCAHONTAS'S WEDDING

In 1607 Captain John Smith (1580–1631), from the English colony of Virginia, was captured by the chief of the Powhatan. Smith's life was dramatically saved by the pleadings of the chief's daughter, Pocahontas (1595–1617). Kidnapped by the English, she met and later married John Rolfe (1585–1622). This marriage kept the peace between the English and the Powhatans until the chief's death in 1618.

TRAPPING FISH

Fish were an important addition to forest game all over the Eastern woodlands, not least because they could be caught all year round. Fish were speared, shot with bows, or taken with hook and line. Where some species migrated upriver to spawn, they could be caught by using nets, weirs, or traps (below).

Loosely woven splint construction

Fish swam into opening but could not turn around once inside

Large handle for carrying awkwardly shaped trap

Powhatan fish trap

TRADITIONAL DRESS

Crowded out of their 17th-century homeland in Pennsylvania and New Jersey by colonial settlement, most Delaware had finally settled in Indian Territory (Oklahoma) by 1830. Traditional dress persisted among women, as seen in this photograph of a mother and daughter from the early 1900s. Nellie Longhat (far right) and her mother are wearing cotton dresses with capes decorated with silver brooches, bead-embroidered moccasins, and an accumulation of bead necklaces.

The Ohio River Valley

THE FERTILE LANDS OF THE GREAT VALLEY drained by the Ohio River
and its many tributaries (from Illinois east to Pennsylvania and south
to Tennessee) offered a rich environment for two great prehistoric
cultures, the Adena and later the Hopewell, which together spanned
about 1500 years to A.D. 500. The Hopewell culture spread from the
Eastern Great Lakes to the Gulf of Mexico and west of the Mississippi. The Hopewell created large burial mounds – almost all
we know about them comes from excavating these earthworks.
Spectacular artists and artisans, they imported exotic raw materials
from a vast trade network. The Hopewell faded as quickly as they
had arisen, and simpler hunter-farmer tribes slowly took their
place. In the 1700s, France and Britain, with their tribal allies,
fought for control of the Ohio Valley as the key to dominating
North America. From the 1790s, relentless white American
settlement created a short-lived intertribal resistance movement
led by the Shawnee statesman Tecumseh.

*Shawnee cloth
storage bag
decorated with
stitching and
appliqué*

*Mother
nursing
a baby*

*Distinctive top-
knot hairstyle
is typically
Hopewell*

*Wrap-round
skirt was usual
garment of Hope-
well women, a style
that continued with
other area tribes
well into the 1800s*

GRAVE IMAGES
The Hopewell people buried their dead surrounded by their
wealth: ornaments, jewelry, fine stone tools, and pottery.
Some of these may have been specially made as grave
objects, like these small clay figurines (above). The burial
sites give us our only knowledge of the Hopewell people's
appearance, clothing, and ornaments, though probably
only of those rich enough to afford large burial mounds.

IN THE BAG
The Shawnee were a powerful force in the
Ohio Valley in the late 1700s. They tried to
become a barrier to American westward
expansion, but they were defeated by
General "Mad Anthony" Wayne in 1794.
In 1831 they sold what was left of their
lands and moved to Oklahoma.

*Tobacco loaded
into bowl in
bird's back*

*Unusual style in
which bird effigy
faces away from
smoker*

STRIKING BIRD
Hopewell stone-carving shows the same
artistry as their other work. Most striking are stone pipes
carved in the shape of animals or birds, such as this raven
(above). Most, called platform pipes, had a base on which
rested the carved figure containing the bowl for tobacco. The
smoker drew the smoke through a hole bored through the base.

Massive stone pipe
found in western
Tennessee

*Smoke drawn
through hole
behind bird's
body*

Decorated Huron sheath made of moose hide

Extensive beadwork

Decorated with 291 nickel-silver brooches

Silk ribbon appliquéd to cloth wrap-around skirt

Colored balls of yarn

HURON HUNTERS
The Huron were long-standing enemies of the Iroquois, who dealt them a stunning defeat in 1649. James Fenimore Cooper (1789–1851), who wrote *The Last of the Mohicans*, made the Iroquois the villains of some of his stories. This Huron skinning-knife sheath is decorated with beads, appliqué stitching, and animal hair.

A POTAWATOMI POUCH
For Native Americans, the great issue of the late 1700s was maintaining the Ohio River as the boundary between white settlers and themselves. Like the Miami and Shawnee, the Potawatomi fought to stop the settlers. After several defeats, they and other tribes signed peace treaties in 1815. Despite hostilities, they traded with whites for new clothing materials, so that only bags, tobacco pouches (above), and moccasins continued to be regularly made from deerskin.

Fine beadwork

MIAMI ALLIANCES
Along with their Ohio Valley allies, the Miami suffered defeats in the 1790s and in the War of 1812. However, trade with whites continued and brought items such as wool, silk ribbon, metal brooches, and glass beads. Miami women used them to add prestige to their clothing and developed techniques to get striking effects, such as the skillful appliqué and nickel-silver decoration on this woolen skirt from the early 1800s.

THE GREAT TECUMSEH
Tecumseh (1768–1813) used his great political skills to forge a tribal alliance opposing white advance into the Midwest. With his shaman twin brother Tenskwatawa (1768–1836), he argued that land could be ceded only with the consent of all the tribes. Despite his belief in peaceful negotiation, in 1811 white forces destroyed the league at the Battle of Tippecanoe (Indiana). Embittered, Tecumseh joined the British (who made him a general) against the U.S. in the War of 1812, in which he was killed.

Western Great Lakes

THE PEOPLES OF THE WESTERN GREAT LAKES (west of Michigan) took full advantage of their access to both woodlands and prairies. In summer the women of tribes such as the Sauk and Fox planted corn and squash while the men hunted buffalo. The Menominee harvested huge quantities of wild rice – their name comes from the Ojibwa name for this plant. In winter the tribes turned to semi-nomadic hunting, living in portable lodges of poles and reed mats as they followed game. The tribes traded with each other, but also were regularly at war. From the early 1600s a powerful force was the Midewiwin, a shaman secret society devoted to healing and encouraging correct behavior as a guarantee of good health.

Male doll given the husband's name, female doll the wife's name

Love medicine is placed in breast of each Menominee doll

Grizzly bear claws separated by triplets of blue beads

MEDICINE DOLLS
Shamans used human figures as "medicine" to control others' behavior. The Menominee used "love dolls" (above) tied face-to-face to ensure that a husband and wife would be faithful to each other. The Potawatomi used dolls as charms to make one person fall in love with another.

SWEET AS MAPLE SUGAR
Maple sugar was greatly valued, used not only on fruit and corn cakes but also as a seasoning on meat and fish. Collection began in late March. Each tree was gashed and a cedarwood spout inserted to allow the sap to drain into a birchbark bucket. Whole Menominee communities moved into the woods, where each family had its own group of trees and a special wigwam.

Ojibwa sap skimmer

Ojibwa wooden trough and Menominee ladle (far left)

MAKING MAPLE SUGAR
First the sap was boiled to reduce its water content. Boiling was done by dropping heated rocks into birchbark containers. After boiling and skimming, the resulting syrup was strained through fiber matting and poured into a wooden trough. As it cooled, it was worked back and forth with a ladle until it formed granules.

SUGAR CONES
Sugar was stored in birchbark containers for use during the year. Some might be forced into molds, such as these Ojibwa cones (right), much like those Europeans used for making conical sugar loaves from cane sugar.

BEAR-CLAW NECKLACE

Necklaces of grizzly bear claws were greatly prized, not least because of the difficulty of persuading their original fearsome owners to part with the main components! Usually the property of a chief or renowned warrior, bear claws were often passed from one generation to another.

CHIEF KEOKUK

Unlike his rival Black Hawk (1767–1838) who fought a hopeless war against settlers in 1832, Sauk chief Keokuk (1780?–1848) realized that his people had to leave Illinois. His tribe honored him for establishing their claim, and that of the politically affiliated Fox, to territory in present-day Iowa. His realism is shown in his avoiding the fate of Black Hawk's followers, destroyed in their war with the U.S. government.

THE SUPERNATURAL

A person who could gain extraordinary power from the spirit world became a shaman. A spirit being, appearing in visions, taught the shaman the uses of many substances (bones, roots, skins), which were stored in a medicine bag (above). Shamans used their power to cure illnesses and to bring success in war and hunting.

Collar made of otter skin

Eagle-feather decoration

Bear-claw necklace of the Fox tribe

Metal bowl held tobacco

WAR OR PEACE PIPE?

Tobacco was thought to have special powers. It was used in offerings to please spirit beings. The Menominee also believed smoking increased their wisdom. At important ceremonies, tribes smoked the sacred calumet, which was passed around clockwise. Because this often marked the end of fighting, the calumet is usually called a peace pipe, but it was also used in the war council.

Sacred Menominee calumet

The settled Southeast

Rᴵᴄʜ ɪɴ ꜰʟᴏʀᴀ ᴀɴᴅ ꜰᴀᴜɴᴀ, with fertile soils and a mild climate, the Southeast was an ideal environment. As skilled builders, artisans, and farmers, with a wide knowledge of medicine, the Southeastern peoples created a flourishing civilization. From A.D. 800 to 1500, the Southeast's Temple Mound Builders developed large towns, traded widely, and held great ceremonies. The rulers lived luxuriously while commoners toiled. The flat-topped mounds seen in the region today are the community sites of this vanished people. The historic Natchez tribe, which also built mounds topped by temples, may have survived the Mound Builders. Contacted by the Europeans in the late 1600s, the Natchez came under pressure from colonists to cede land but fought back. Three wars with the French in the 1700s destroyed their nation, scattering the survivors throughout the Southeast.

Map of North America showing the Southeast region

THE ANNUAL BUSK
The Green Corn Ceremony (Busk) was the most important rite of the Southeast. It was held when the corn ripened, offering thanks for the harvest and marking the beginning of a new year. It involved ritual purification, dancing around a sacred fire, and a celebratory feast.

Yuchi (of Tennessee) feather fan carried by dancers

Thatched roof

Pole frame

Sleeping platform

Mud wall

Model of a Natchez house

Color of fan echoed color of Busk – spectators and dancers alike were dressed in white

SUNS AND STINKARDS
Successor to the Temple Mound Builders, the Natchez (of Louisiana) amazed French explorers with their complex hierarchical society and elaborate ceremonies. Ruled by an all-powerful monarch, the Great Sun, Natchez society was divided into Suns, nobles, honored men, and commoners (stinkards). The main village had houses such as the one above, and on a mound, a temple that sheltered an eternal flame.

Wooden lacrosse stick measured up to 3 ft (1 m) long

A TWO-HANDLED, THREE-LEGGED POT
Women made the pottery in the Southeast. The clay was cleaned and mixed, and long clay cylinders were layered on top of a small clay disk. A wetted shell was used to smooth the clay, thin the walls, and shape the pot. Before firing, the pot was polished with a smooth pebble and designs cut in with a pointed wooden tool.

Finely etched decoration

Catawba (of South Carolina) pot based on ancient techniques

SHELL GORGET
.The Temple Mound people often used decoratively incised shells as ornaments. This gorget (a plate hung around the neck to rest on the chest) has the image of a long-nosed god. Unfortunately, because these people had no writing, our knowledge of their beliefs is fragmentary.

Skin-covered Yuchi lacrosse ball stitched together with sinew

Hole for string to allow gorget to be hung from neck

Loosely woven webbing made of thin strips of hide

Perfectly rounded chunkey disk made of highly polished stone

Heavily woven webbing showing more intricate style

A CHUNKEY STONE
A popular Temple Mound Builders sport was "chunkey." One player rolled a polished stone disk down a court 100 ft (30 m) long. Then he and his opponent threw wooden lances to mark where they guessed the disk would fall over. The game was still played in the Southeast when the Europeans arrived.

HOW TO PLAY LACROSSE
Known to many Native North American peoples, the stick-and-ball game that French explorers called lacrosse was played with fanatical enthusiasm in the Southeast. Teams had 100 players each, often many more. Each player used two sticks with webbed ends to catch and throw a ball made of wood or stuffed deerskin, ultimately aiming to hurl it between the opposing team's goalposts.

Each stick is made of a single piece of bent wood

Thin strips of hide lash the two ends together

Each player is allowed to hold two lacrosse sticks

Special designs painted on face and body

Mane worn around neck

Beaded belt

Yuchi lacrosse stick

DRAMATIC PAINTINGS
American artist George Catlin (1796–1872) painted several dramatic pictures of lacrosse in 1834. This portrait shows Thirsts-for-Stone, an outstanding Choctaw (of Mississippi) lacrosse player, wearing his best game outfit (right). He would have drunk sacred medicine and performed ritual dances before the game. The women of the village, accompanied by medicine men, sought aid from the spirit world for their team through dances and song.

Long, rigid horsetail

George Catlin painting of a Choctaw ball game

LITTLE BROTHER OF WAR
Lacrosse as played in the Southeast was so violent that the Indians called it the "little brother of war." Serious injuries were commonplace and players sometimes were killed. Challenge matches between villages or tribes drew perhaps a thousand rival supporters. Spectators bet heavily on the result.

The "Five Civilized Tribes"

A REMARKABLE CIVILIZATION had grown up in the lush Southeast by the late 1500s. The tribes lived in planned villages, were skilled farmers as well as hunters, and had advanced medical knowledge. Three hundred years later they had adopted American agricultural methods and had put their laws in written form. Many had become Christians. All this made no difference to the whites, who were determined to seize their tribal lands. In the 1830s, the Choctaw, followed by the Cherokee, Chickasaw, Creek, and finally Seminole (called the "Five Civilized Tribes" by the whites), were forcibly moved to Oklahoma. Many died on the trail.

Fine beadwork fit for a chief

DRESSING UP
Seminole dolls show how women, up to the early 1900s, combed their hair around a frame and wore skirts and capes of strips of cotton cloth in contrasting colors. A girl was given a string of beads when young and added strings throughout her life, until they almost reached her ears – and weighed several pounds.

THE EAGLE DANCE
Before contact with Europeans, a most important Cherokee ceremony was the Eagle Dance, held as part of the rites celebrating both peace and war. Dancers wore eagle feathers on their heads and waved eagle-feather wands to the music of drums and rattles.

Smaller feathers attached with sinew to both ends of wooden handle

CHIEF OF THE CHOCTAW
The Choctaws' home was in Mississippi and Louisiana, until most were removed by the U.S. government to a reservation in Indian Territory, which was later called Oklahoma (the Choctaw name for "red people"). A chief of those Choctaw who managed to stay in Louisiana wore this sash at his wedding in 1871.

Feathers decorate Cherokee Eagle Dance wand

Small entrance leading into windowless house

A LITTLE HUT BY THE WATER
In hot, humid Florida, such as the Everglades swamps, the Seminole lived in open-sided dwellings (chickees). Made from palmetto poles with thatched roofs, these huts were built on platforms to avoid flooding from the heavy rains.

Wall made of dried mud smoothed onto gatelike framework of small poles

26

MAKING MUSIC

Southeastern ceremonies and games were accompanied by music made by drums and rattles. A water drum had a deerskin stretched over a hollow log containing water so that it resonated. Rattles were made from dried turtle shells, cattle horns, or gourds.

Creek rattle made of hollowed-out gourd filled with corn kernels or small stones to make sounds

Conical roof made up of several poles running from the circumference at the bottom of the structure

THE UNDEFEATED SEMINOLE

Originally mostly Creek from Georgia and Alabama, the Seminole (left) fled to Florida (their name means "runaway") in the 1700s, where they were joined by many runaway slaves. The Seminole fought two wars with the U.S. The second (1835–42) began with the government's efforts to remove them to Oklahoma. Led by the great Osceola (below), the Seminole fought U.S. forces to a standstill. Although many Seminole surrendered in 1841–42 and were sent west, others remained in Florida's Everglades swamps, undefeated. A treaty was signed with them only in 1934, ending possibly the longest war in history.

George Catlin painting of Osceola

A MEETING HOUSE

Creek village dwellings were carefully organized into cool summer houses and warm winter lodges. In summer the Council of Elders met in a square surrounded by sun shelters, and in a round house up to 25 ft (7.5 m) high in bad weather. This council house was also used for ceremonies and festivities.

SEMINOLE HERO

In 1835, enraged by an agreement to move the Seminole to Oklahoma, Osceola (1804–38) killed a rival chief to become leader of those who were determined to stay in their Florida homeland. Small bands of guerrilla forces were led by Osceola against 10,000 U.S. troops until he was captured through a dishonorable false truce.

Roof made of thin tree trunks, covered with bark sheeting to provide extra protection from heavy rains

Central fire

Model of Creek council house in which elders are holding a meeting

The Great Plains

A SEA OF GRASS stretched more than 2,000 miles (3,200 km) north to south between the Rocky Mountains and the Mississippi River. In 1800 this area supported about 150,000 people and 60 million buffalo, all sharing 1 million sq miles (2.5 million sq km) of territory. With sparse rainfall on the western Plains, tribes there were dependent on the huge herds of buffalo, unlike tribes of the better-watered eastern prairie, who combined farming with buffalo hunting. Buffalo migrations dictated the way of living for the 30 Plains tribes. The buffalo meant not just a crucial source of meat – their hides, hair, and horns made dwellings, clothing, tools, and utensils. Before the Spanish brought horses to the Southwest in the 1500s, nomadic Plains tribes traveled and hunted on foot. Of all Native North Americans, Plains peoples were the finest horsemen. Their riding skills dominated the style of their incessant warfare.

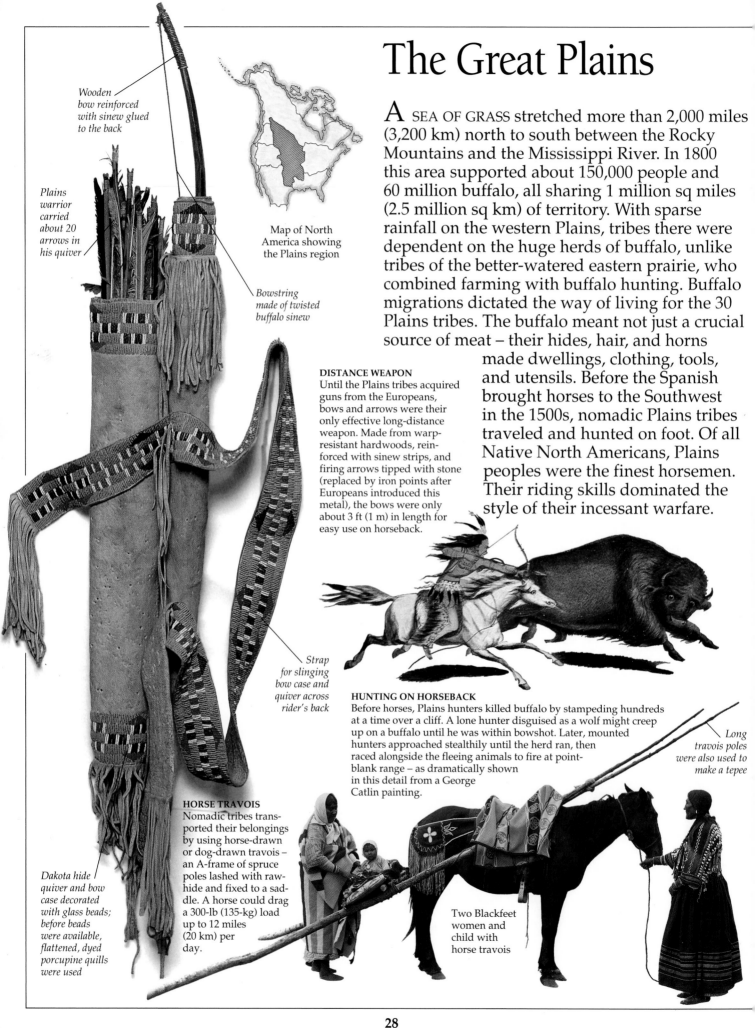

Wooden bow reinforced with sinew glued to the back

Plains warrior carried about 20 arrows in his quiver

Map of North America showing the Plains region

Bowstring made of twisted buffalo sinew

DISTANCE WEAPON
Until the Plains tribes acquired guns from the Europeans, bows and arrows were their only effective long-distance weapon. Made from warp-resistant hardwoods, reinforced with sinew strips, and firing arrows tipped with stone (replaced by iron points after Europeans introduced this metal), the bows were only about 3 ft (1 m) in length for easy use on horseback.

Strap for slinging bow case and quiver across rider's back

HORSE TRAVOIS
Nomadic tribes transported their belongings by using horse-drawn or dog-drawn travois – an A-frame of spruce poles lashed with rawhide and fixed to a saddle. A horse could drag a 300-lb (135-kg) load up to 12 miles (20 km) per day.

Dakota hide quiver and bow case decorated with glass beads; before beads were available, flattened, dyed porcupine quills were used

HUNTING ON HORSEBACK
Before horses, Plains hunters killed buffalo by stampeding hundreds at a time over a cliff. A lone hunter disguised as a wolf might creep up on a buffalo until he was within bowshot. Later, mounted hunters approached stealthily until the herd ran, then raced alongside the fleeing animals to fire at point-blank range – as dramatically shown in this detail from a George Catlin painting.

Long travois poles were also used to make a tepee

Two Blackfeet women and child with horse travois

PLAINS BALL GAME
The Plains peoples played games that tested qualities important to their way of life, such as speed and strength. The most popular game among women was shinny. Two teams armed with curved or straight sticks struggled to get the ball (below) past each other's goalposts. The ball could be batted or kicked but not touched with the hand. Men also played, and sometimes a men's team might challenge a women's.

Each pole up to 25 ft (7.5 m) long

Smoke flap adjusts to keep heat in or to air out tepee

Arapaho-decorated hide ball used in game of shinny

HAVE TEPEE WILL TRAVEL
For the nomadic hunting tribes, the tepee was a highly practical dwelling, cool in summer and warm in winter. Constructed from a cone of long poles covered with buffalo hides sewn together, it could be erected by two women in an hour. About 15 ft (5 m) in diameter, it comfortably housed a family, their bedding, and their belongings. Tepees were usually decorated with traditional painted designs.

Design painted on Blackfeet tepee could come from mythical dream creatures, such as an otter

Two sticks used in a Plains Cree throwing game

Up to 20 straight poles bound together at top formed cone shape

Arrow with eagle's feather denotes lightning

Entire crow belt represents the Thunderbird spirit being

Feathers represent birds of prey fighting over dead bodies in war

Buffalo hide (from 8 to 20 skins) draped over pole skeleton

Wooden lodge pins removed when tepee folded up for traveling

Bells represent sound of thunder

Model of Arapaho Grass Dancer

GRASS DANCE
In the late 1800s a new ceremony, the Grass Dance, spread throughout the Plains tribes. Originally an Omaha ritual that recalled men's courage and achievements in war, it became a social dance with songs and costumes. To a people threatened with the destruction of their way of life, the Grass Dance became, and remains, a symbol of Native North American solidarity.

Tepee set up with entrance facing east, because of prevailing westerly winds

The Dakota (Sioux)

THE LORDS OF THE NORTHERN PLAINS by the mid-1800s were the Dakota, called Sioux by Europeans (from an Ojibwa word for "enemy"). In the 1700s they had been forced westward by well-armed Ojibwa from their Western Great Lakes homeland. The Dakota were made up of seven independent groups, ranging from Minnesota west to the Upper Missouri River. The largest of the Plains tribes and outstanding warriors, the Dakota terrorized their Indian enemies and offered fierce resistance to whites. Their lives depended on the buffalo – and the end of the great herds meant the end of their independence. Between 1862 and 1877 they forcefully resisted the U.S. advance into their lands. In 1876, in eastern Montana near the Little Bighorn River, they inflicted on the U.S. Army the most famous defeat by Native North Americans.

USING A BOW AND ARROW
Dakota children were taught proper behavior and encouraged to imitate adults. They were treated with much affection and rarely punished. They were expected, however, to learn skills at a young age. Boys practiced shooting with half-sized bows and arrows (above), first at targets, then at small game, and began hunting seriously in their early teens. Girls were expected to help their mothers in strenuous outside work.

Geometric beadwork style was favored by the Dakota

BETTER THAN BAREBACK
Though Plains tribes long rode bareback, a saddle and stirrups gave better stability and control. The Dakota "pad saddle" was made from two pieces of tanned hide stitched together and stuffed with buffalo or deer hair. It had hardly any cantle to support the rider's back, or pommel at the front. Stirrups, usually wooden, were attached by a rawhide strap.

Unadorned fringed central flap

Flank strap (cinch) of heavy cotton

Hide strap for tying items to saddle

Buffalo raw-hide covers wooden stirrup

Detail from 1881 pictograph of the Battle of the Little Bighorn, painted on a buffalo hide (below)

THE BATTLE OF THE LITTLE BIGHORN
Gold seekers invading the sacred Black Hills in South Dakota, guaranteed to the Dakota by treaty, brought about war in 1876. A U.S. Army unit moved against a huge force of Dakota and Cheyenne, not realizing their numbers. General George A. Custer (1839–76) impetuously attacked with an advance guard. On June 25, 1876, he and his 215 men were all killed.

DEATH ON THE PLAINS
The Dakota did not bury their dead. Instead, the body was wrapped in a buffalo robe and placed beyond the reach of wild animals on a platform supported by poles. Warriors had their weapons and medicine pouch hung beside them, women their important household utensils. Relatives mourned beside the body.

Unusual warfare design

Lance with beadwork, buffalo fur, horsehair, and feathers

Eagle-feather headdress

Horsehair tassel

Porcupine quills were dyed and flattened before being sewn with sinew onto hide bag

THE ART OF QUILLWORK
Before white traders arrived with beads, Plains women took great pride in their quilling skills. Women's saddlebags were made in pairs to hang on each side of a saddle or to store household articles in a tepee.

OLD MAN OF THE PLAINS
Ceremonial dress for a Dakota elder in the mid-1800s marked his status. His headdress of eagle tail feathers (thought to have spirit power) could be worn only by a proven warrior. His costume was completed by bear paws, beaded leggings, and quilled moccasins. A headdress such as this was presented to Sitting Bull when he became a chief of the Teton Dakota.

Elaborately beaded cradleboard with metal stud, horseshoe, and bell decoration

Poncho-style shirt, made of mountain sheep skin, is painted blue and yellow and has scalplocks and quillwork

SITTING BULL
A medicine man who was chosen principal chief of the Teton Dakota in 1868, Sitting Bull (1834?–90) displayed great qualities of leadership. In 1876, with Chief Crazy Horse (1849?–77), he united the Dakota to fight the U.S. army and succeeded in destroying Custer's unit. Later pardoned, he starred in the Wild West Show of Buffalo Bill (William Cody, 1846–1917).

CRADLE WILL ROCK
A Dakota baby spent much of its time in a cradleboard. A lace-up skin bag on a wooden framework, it could be strapped to a mother's back, hung from a saddle, tied to a travois, or just propped upright. A decorated cradleboard like this would usually be made by the sister of the baby's father.

Mandan and Hidatsa

FERTILE RIVER VALLEYS and open prairies, hot summers and numbingly cold winters – the Mandan and Hidatsa learned to adapt to and exploit their homeland on the upper Missouri River in North Dakota. They built permanent earth-lodge villages on the high banks above the river and farmed the bottom lands. Half of their food came from crops such as corn, the rest from the vital summer buffalo hunt. To deal with winter cold, they built separate lodges along the river, where there was plenty of wood for fuel. As hunter-farmers the Mandan and Hidatsa were typical of the prairie tribes, just as the Dakota were typical of the high plains tribes. They were fierce warriors, which was necessary to protect themselves from marauding bands of Dakota.

Model of a bullboat, a circular skin-covered vessel

ACROSS THE RIVER
Settled on the Plains rivers, the Mandan used bullboats. Made from a (bull) buffalo hide stretched over a willow frame-work, a bullboat was light but strong enough to carry heavy loads. Able to move in very shallow water, it was usually a one-person craft. The paddler knelt in front and dipped the paddle straight down. To prevent the boat from spinning, the buffalo's tail was left on. Attached to a piece of wood, it acted as a stabilizer.

BRAIDED EARS
Raising crops was women's work, but men sometimes helped clear land or harvest the crops. A Plains woman, helped by her female kin, could farm 3 acres (1.2 ha) each year. She grew corn, beans, squash, sun-flowers, and melon. Planting was done in spring and har-vesting in September, when the ears of corn were husked (outer leaves of cobs removed). The best ears were braided into strings, hung up to dry, then stored in pits in the floor of the earth lodge.

INSIDE A MANDAN LODGE
In 1833–34 a German prince, Maximilian von Wied-Neuwied, toured the American West to study the tribes. To make a visual record of his findings, the prince took Swiss painter Karl Bodmer (1809–93) on the trip. They traveled far up the Missouri River and met the Mandan and Hidatsa tribes. Bodmer's painting (left) of the interior of a Mandan lodge shows warriors, with horses, dogs, and weapons to hand, viewed by the dim light of the chimney hole.

Chimney hole, covered by bullboat frame-work, lets in light

CLOSE TO THE EARTH
Earth lodges were dome-shaped, up to 50 ft (15 m) wide. Built mainly by women, they were home to their extended families, together with horses, dogs, and belongings. An earth lodge was thought to be sacred, and its construction was accompanied by many ceremonies. All social activities and house-keeping took place around a central fireplace.

Roof of wooden rafters topped with willows, grass, and sod

Entrance was a covered walkway with an inner skin door

Carved knife in horned eagle-feather headdress represents a battle with a Cheyenne chief

Karl Bodmer's portrait of Four Bears – the last great Mandan chief

CHIEF FOUR BEARS
Prince Maximilian believed the Mandan were descendants of the Welsh prince Madoc, who supposedly sailed to America in 1170 – a tale long proved to be false! During the winter of 1833–34, so cold that his paints froze, Karl Bodmer produced several fine pictures, including this portrait of the Mandan chief Mato-Tope (Four Bears). Mato-Tope must have become used to posing for a portrait, since the artist George Catlin (1796–1872) had painted him the previous year.

Antler horns tied to wooden handle by animal sinew

Wooden hide-covered handle

Hammer made by covering a round stone with buffalo hide

INVALUABLE KNOWLEDGE
The story of the Hidatsa has been strikingly told by Buffalo Bird Woman (1839–1920s?) and her son, Edward Goodbird (1869–1938), who were photographed with Son of a Star (right) in 1906. Much of their story was related to an anthropologist (someone who studies cultures) working in collaboration with the American Museum of Natural History. Besides invaluable knowledge of tribal life and customs, their account detailed the move to a government reservation (1885–88) and the problems this brought.

MAKING PEMMICAN
Pemmican was the all-purpose emergency food of the Plains, with a very long shelf life. It was made by mixing dried buffalo meat, boiled fat, and chokecherries (bitter berries from local shrubs). For pounding the meat until it was nearly powder and for cracking the bones to boil out the fat, a large stone hammer was used. Pemmican was very nutritious and would keep for years.

Canopy, made from half a tepee cover, provided privacy in the sleeping area

Sacred shrine was located opposite the entrance at the rear of the lodge

A SIGN OF THE TINES
For weeding the fields of corn, the Hidatsa preferred rakes with deer antler tines (prongs). This was partly because they believed wooden rakes produced the worms that damaged the corn crop. Tribal stories told of deer weeding the garden of their ancestor, Eternal Grandmother, and of how she made the first rakes from their cast-off antlers.

War and peace

On the Great Plains, warfare was part of life but it rarely involved great battles between tribes. Instead, small bands of warriors made raids to steal horses or to avenge a death – and always to win honor. Audacity and courage were greatly respected and deeds were graded on a system of "coups" (the French word for blows), which included taking a scalp, stealing a horse, or touching an enemy in battle. War was a bloody and deadly business that inflicted serious casualties on each tribe. Tribal warfare was a test of personal courage and spiritual power, rather than a battle for territory and political control conducted by disciplined soldiers. Native North American war customs left them at a great disadvantage when fighting white and black regiments.

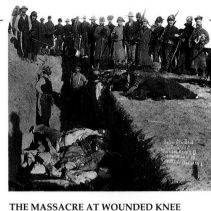

THE MASSACRE AT WOUNDED KNEE
In the turmoil created by the Ghost Dance (below left), on December 29, 1890, 470 7th Cavalry troopers were guarding 340 surrendered Sioux. A tense situation exploded and both sides opened fire. Over 64 soldiers and 200 Sioux (including unarmed women and children) were killed. The Sioux bodies were dumped into a mass grave. Wounded Knee became a symbol to Native North Americans of their mistreatment by whites.

Metal blade fitted around wooden handle

Carved face is symbol of owner's supernatural helper, who appeared in Ghost Dance vision

WAR PARTY
A Plains raiding party was armed with bows and arrows, shields, lances, clubs, and scalping knives. A war club might have a blade, spike, or shaped stone at the top. Tomahawk-pipes, like this Dakota example, were used more as prestigious ceremonial objects than as weapons.

Wand made from wooden tube or hollow reed

Arapaho Ghost Dance wand

Headdress is a circle of magpie and turkey feathers

Wand with white shaft and mottled feathers represents the female calumet

VISION OF HOPE
By the late 1800s, the Plains peoples, in despair on reservations, turned to a new ceremony, the Ghost Dancer. Born in a Paiute prophet's (Wovoka, pp. 40–41) vision, it promised the end of the whites and a return of the buffalo. Soon Ghost Dancers sought visions in which they visited the spirit world and met dead relatives. In later dances, they carried objects seen in the visions (left).

DOG SOCIETIES
Various Plains tribes, such as the Blackfeet, Hidatsa, and Gros Ventre, had a military Dog Society. On a tour of the West in 1833–34, Swiss artist Karl Bodmer painted this striking portrait of a Hidatsa Dog Dancer, Pehriska-Ruhpa (Two Ravens). Hidatsa Dogs were "contraries" and did everything backward – for example, if a warrior was meant to attack in battle, he was told to flee.

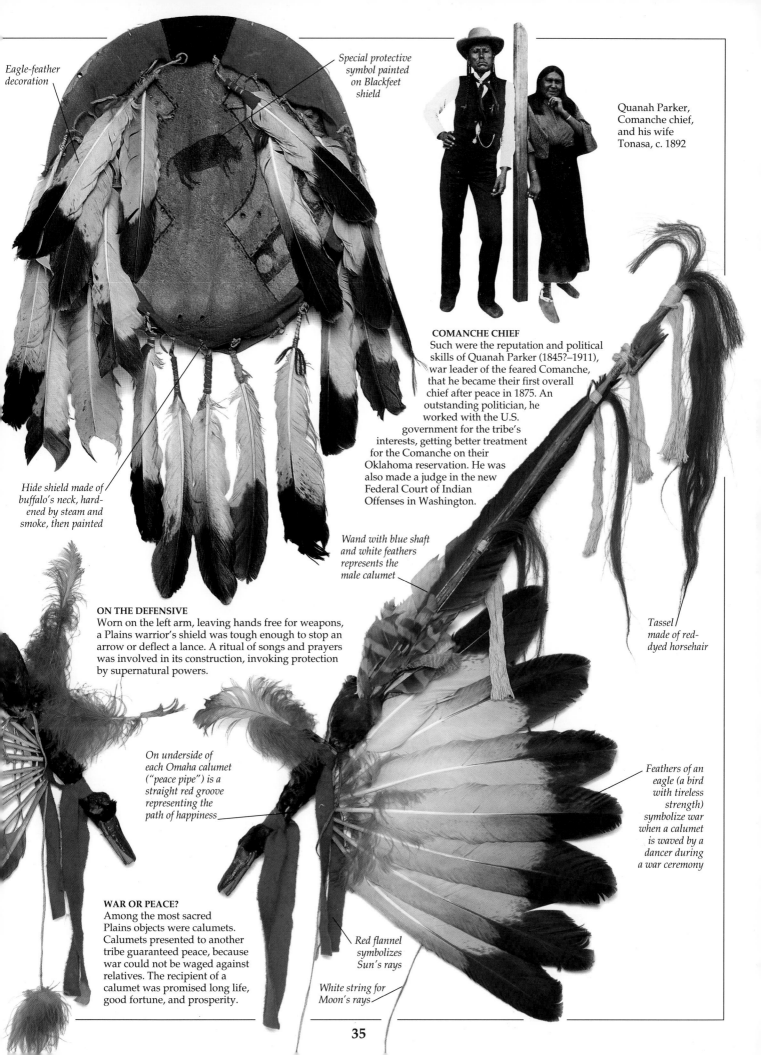

Eagle-feather decoration

Special protective symbol painted on Blackfeet shield

Quanah Parker, Comanche chief, and his wife Tonasa, c. 1892

COMANCHE CHIEF
Such were the reputation and political skills of Quanah Parker (1845?–1911), war leader of the feared Comanche, that he became their first overall chief after peace in 1875. An outstanding politician, he worked with the U.S. government for the tribe's interests, getting better treatment for the Comanche on their Oklahoma reservation. He was also made a judge in the new Federal Court of Indian Offenses in Washington.

Hide shield made of buffalo's neck, hardened by steam and smoke, then painted

Wand with blue shaft and white feathers represents the male calumet

Tassel made of red-dyed horsehair

ON THE DEFENSIVE
Worn on the left arm, leaving hands free for weapons, a Plains warrior's shield was tough enough to stop an arrow or deflect a lance. A ritual of songs and prayers was involved in its construction, invoking protection by supernatural powers.

On underside of each Omaha calumet ("peace pipe") is a straight red groove representing the path of happiness

Feathers of an eagle (a bird with tireless strength) symbolize war when a calumet is waved by a dancer during a war ceremony

WAR OR PEACE?
Among the most sacred Plains objects were calumets. Calumets presented to another tribe guaranteed peace, because war could not be waged against relatives. The recipient of a calumet was promised long life, good fortune, and prosperity.

Red flannel symbolizes Sun's rays

White string for Moon's rays

The Sun Dance

Aт тне тιме of the summer buffalo hunt, when each tribe had reunited after scattering widely in the winter, most Plains peoples held the Sun Dance – the greatest of their ceremonies. The rites differed among tribes such as the Dakota, Crow, and Blackfeet, but the purpose was to thank the Great Spirit for past help and pray for future blessings. The ceremony fulfilled a promise by one person (a pledger) to show gratitude for aid from the spirit world, although it was for the benefit of the whole tribe. The ritual lasted several days and nights. Tribes built a sacred Sun Dance Lodge, where a sacred cottonwood tree, forked at the top, was at the center of the ceremony. Found by a warrior, it had been cut down by specially chosen virtuous women. The days of ritual dances ended with several kinds of ordeal. Volunteers chose to accept self-imposed pain in order to have a personal vision. It was also hoped that the Great Spirit would spare the whole tribe from future suffering.

Slow Bull, a Plains medicine man

Buffalo skull specially painted and placed at the altar of the Blackfeet Sun Dance

THE GREAT SPIRIT
The Plains world was filled with spirits who possessed power and inhabited places, persons, animals, even objects. Some tribes believed all power came from the Great Spirit. Individuals might sing to lesser spirits to plead for their aid, or by privation seek a vision that would transmit to them some sacred power. Those who gained great power became "medicine men," tribal leaders and advisers.

Feather headdress adorning Dakota effigy

MOST POWERFUL MEDICINE
The Crow Sun Dance was held for someone seeking vengeance for the killing of a relative. A ceremonial doll was suspended by a hoop from the sacred cottonwood. Crow sacred stories tell of a warrior grieving for his family, who were killed by enemies. A vision showed him how to make the doll, which would ensure revenge.

Feather headdress decorated with fur and beads

SACRED EFFIGIES
The Dakota attached special objects to the fork of the sacred cottonwood in the Sun Dance Lodge as the focus for a ritual dance. These objects, made of raw-hide, were effigies (symbolic figures). They were simple cut-out figures of a man (symbolizing the enemy) and a buffalo. The ritual ended with dancers firing arrows at the figures.

Simple buffalo effigy cut from a piece of rawhide

Crow deerskin doll is stuffed with sweetgrass

RESPECT FOR BUFFALO
As the vital resource at the center of their way of life, the buffalo was featured prominently by most Plains people in their versions of the Sun Dance. Both Blackfeet and Dakota painted buffalo skulls and decorated them with sage and grass.

Cylindrical case for storing the Blackfeet Natoas bundle, which included a sacred headdress

Digging stick

Eye and nose cavities were stuffed with sage and grass, as a symbolic offering to the buffalo to wish them successful grazing

Rawhide fringing

Detail from a painting by Frederic Remington (1861–1909)

AN AGONIZING ORDEAL
In the Sun Dance ordeal, all dancers fasted and endured privations. But some chose to have rawhide thongs driven through their chest muscles on wooden skewers and attached to the fork of the sacred cottonwood pole. Swaying to the music and blowing eagle-bone whistles, or even suspended from the fork, they gained release only when the skewers tore out of their flesh. Disturbed by this practice, the U.S. government banned the entire Sun Dance from 1904 to 1935.

A SACRED WOMAN
In addition to cutting down the sacred cottonwood tree, women sang during the various dances, brought the dancers presents, and took part in the ordeals. But most important, the Blackfeet ceremony depended on a Sacred Woman for the rituals. Whoever had pledged the Sun Dance had to buy a Natoas bundle, and it was transferred to the Sacred Woman in a special rite. Kept in a rawhide case, the Natoas bundle contained several sacred objects, such as face paints and rattles, but the most important were a headdress and a digging stick.

The high Plateau

THE GREAT PLATEAU, west of the northern Plains, was home to 25 tribes. It stretched from the Rockies westward to the Cascade Mountains of Oregon, and from the Fraser River south to Idaho and western Wyoming. Most tribes lived in tepee-like lodges in summer, and in winter, earth-covered, part-underground houses. Their main food was salmon and edible roots. Some tribes became traders and bartered skins, hemp, and horn bows for buffalo skins, superior robes, and decorated objects from the Plains. The Plateau peoples began using horses only in the 1700s but soon became famous for breeding and trading them. Trade brought prosperity, which ended only with pressure from white expansion after the 1830s.

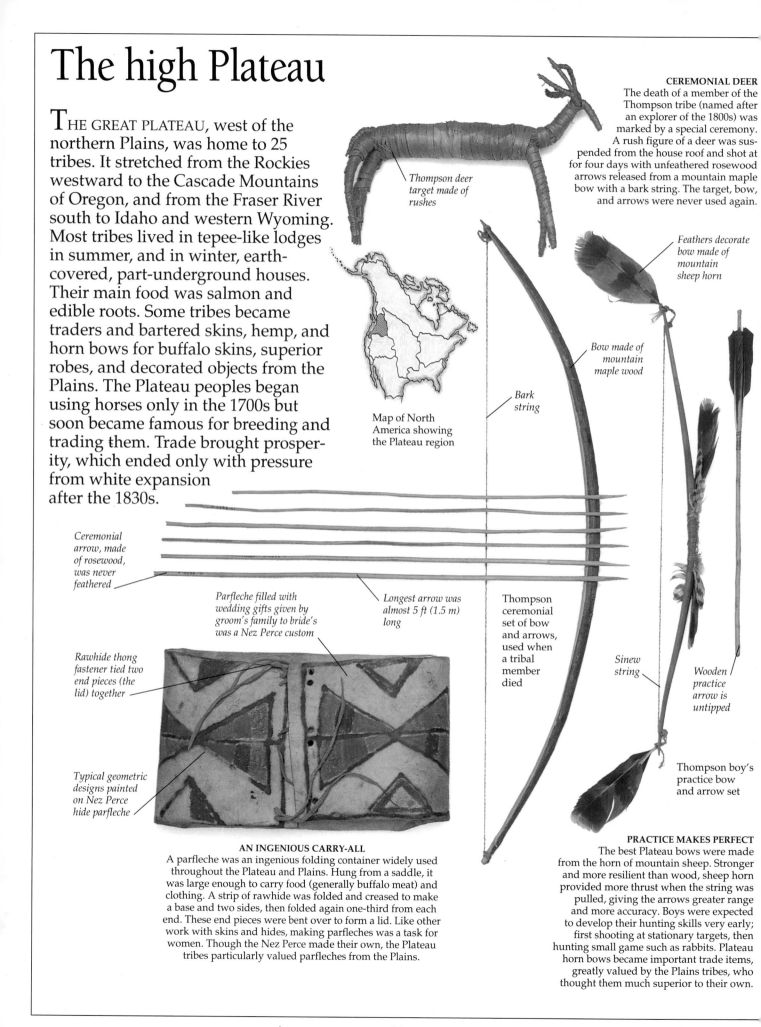

Thompson deer target made of rushes

CEREMONIAL DEER
The death of a member of the Thompson tribe (named after an explorer of the 1800s) was marked by a special ceremony. A rush figure of a deer was suspended from the house roof and shot at for four days with unfeathered rosewood arrows released from a mountain maple bow with a bark string. The target, bow, and arrows were never used again.

Feathers decorate bow made of mountain sheep horn

Bow made of mountain maple wood

Bark string

Map of North America showing the Plateau region

Ceremonial arrow, made of rosewood, was never feathered

Parfleche filled with wedding gifts given by groom's family to bride's was a Nez Perce custom

Longest arrow was almost 5 ft (1.5 m) long

Thompson ceremonial set of bow and arrows, used when a tribal member died

Sinew string

Rawhide thong fastener tied two end pieces (the lid) together

Wooden practice arrow is untipped

Typical geometric designs painted on Nez Perce hide parfleche

Thompson boy's practice bow and arrow set

AN INGENIOUS CARRY-ALL
A parfleche was an ingenious folding container widely used throughout the Plateau and Plains. Hung from a saddle, it was large enough to carry food (generally buffalo meat) and clothing. A strip of rawhide was folded and creased to make a base and two sides, then folded again one-third from each end. These end pieces were bent over to form a lid. Like other work with skins and hides, making parfleches was a task for women. Though the Nez Perce made their own, the Plateau tribes particularly valued parfleches from the Plains.

PRACTICE MAKES PERFECT
The best Plateau bows were made from the horn of mountain sheep. Stronger and more resilient than wood, sheep horn provided more thrust when the string was pulled, giving the arrows greater range and more accuracy. Boys were expected to develop their hunting skills very early; first shooting at stationary targets, then hunting small game such as rabbits. Plateau horn bows became important trade items, greatly valued by the Plains tribes, who thought them much superior to their own.

*Red and black
geometric
design
appliquéd to
Thompson
hide saddlebag*

THE GREAT CHASE
Clashes with whites escalated into the Nez Perce War of 1877. The band of Chief Joseph (c. 1840–1904) fought a series of running battles with increasingly larger forces of the U.S. Cavalry and local volunteers. The Nez Perce consistently outfought their enemies in a chase lasting four months and covering over 1,600 miles (2,600 km), until they were forced to surrender only 30 miles (48 km) short of sanctuary in Canada.

Chief Joseph

A REVOLUTION
The horse revolutionized the Plateau peoples' way of life. It extended the range of their summer migrations and spread their trade down into California and deep into the Plains. As a result, they brought back not only bartered goods but many of their neighbors' customs. However, they did not adopt the Plains travois for transport. Instead they used pack saddles and saddlebags, such as this double one from the Thompson tribe, who lived in southern British Columbia.

*Antler
spike*

RAIDING PARTY
The Thompson tribe used to raid their neighbors for booty, revenge, and honor, much like most Native North American peoples. This two-handed war club is crudely decorated, showing a lake with three warriors nearby. The notches at each end were probably ornamental but may have been for tallying numbers of enemy killed, just as Western gunfighters were alleged to notch their guns.

*Thompson
birchwood war
club, also used
for hunting
beaver*

*Hide
fringing*

IN THE BAG
The Nez Perce were famous for their corn-husk bags. Made of twisted hemp fiber, twined without using a loom, the bags were decorated with cords made from the inner parts of cornhusks. Cords were dyed with colors made of natural materials to produce typical geometric designs, with a different design appearing on the reverse side of the bag. Flexible, flat containers, cornhusk bags were used to carry foodstuffs, roots, and berries. After horses, they were the Nez Perce's most important trade goods.

*Each notch
perhaps
denoted an
enemy or
beaver that
had been killed
with this club*

The Great Basin

A BAKING DESERT IN SUMMER, lashed by storms and snow in winter, the Great Basin has always had meager resources. Nine tribes, scattered over 400,000 sq miles (1 million sq km), had adapted so well to their environment that their way of life endured for some 10,000 years. Without agriculture, and living on wild foods ranging from insects and seeds to lizards and deer, the ingenuity of these migratory people is easy to miss. They needed no permanent homes, as they migrated with the seasons, gathering in large encampments during pine nut harvests and rabbit drives. After gold was discovered here in 1859, their lives changed drastically.

Map of North America showing the Great Basin – Nevada, Utah, Idaho, Oregon, Wyoming, and Colorado

FAMOUS BASKET WEAVER
The Great Basin tribes were expert basket weavers, particularly the Washoe, whose products were greatly valued by white buyers. Datsolali (1835?–1925) was the most famous of all Native American basket weavers. Her baskets showed control of difficult shapes and displayed traditional patterns involving extrafine stitching.

Nevada Washoe basket-maker Datsolali (white name, Louisa Keyser)

PAIUTE PROPHET
In 1888 a Nevada Paiute shaman, Wovoka (white name Jack Wilson, 1856?–1932), began to prophesy that by using a new ceremony (the Ghost Dance, which spread rapidly to the Plains), the white man would be swept away, the buffalo returned, and the old ways restored. Though his message stressed nonviolence, the white authorities reacted with brutality.

UTE BEADWORK
The Ute homeland was on the edge of the Plains, so they adopted the neotraditional Plains ceremonial costume. This combined a European-style garment with imported glass beads decorated in traditional designs (right). White pressure soon destroyed their hunting and raiding way of life. By the 1870s most Utes had been forced onto reservations.

Cloth strip edging garment shows white influence in style, although basic material is deerskin

Colored beads forming geometric design show fine craftwork of this Ute child's coat

Northern Paiute duck decoy made from bundles of tule reed

Plant fiber ties

Deerhide fringing

DUCK DECOY
The Northern Paiute of northwestern Nevada hunted any game available, including rabbits and marmots. In the spring, migrating birds, such as ducks, were hunted with the help of duck-shaped decoys made from bulrush (tule) bundles tied together with rush fiber. Floating realistically on reed marshes within range of the hidden hunters' bows, they convinced the ducks it was safe to land.

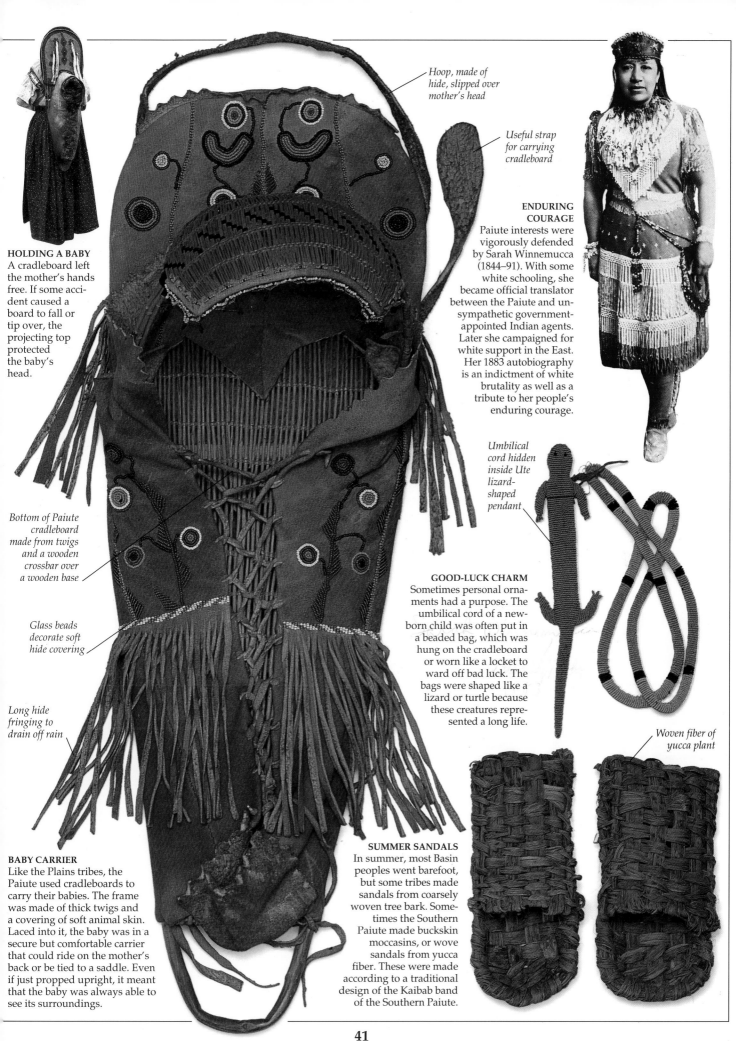

HOLDING A BABY
A cradleboard left the mother's hands free. If some accident caused a board to fall or tip over, the projecting top protected the baby's head.

Hoop, made of hide, slipped over mother's head

Useful strap for carrying cradleboard

ENDURING COURAGE
Paiute interests were vigorously defended by Sarah Winnemucca (1844–91). With some white schooling, she became official translator between the Paiute and unsympathetic government-appointed Indian agents. Later she campaigned for white support in the East. Her 1883 autobiography is an indictment of white brutality as well as a tribute to her people's enduring courage.

Bottom of Paiute cradleboard made from twigs and a wooden crossbar over a wooden base

Glass beads decorate soft hide covering

Umbilical cord hidden inside Ute lizard-shaped pendant

GOOD-LUCK CHARM
Sometimes personal ornaments had a purpose. The umbilical cord of a newborn child was often put in a beaded bag, which was hung on the cradleboard or worn like a locket to ward off bad luck. The bags were shaped like a lizard or turtle because these creatures represented a long life.

Long hide fringing to drain off rain

Woven fiber of yucca plant

BABY CARRIER
Like the Plains tribes, the Paiute used cradleboards to carry their babies. The frame was made of thick twigs and a covering of soft animal skin. Laced into it, the baby was in a secure but comfortable carrier that could ride on the mother's back or be tied to a saddle. Even if just propped upright, it meant that the baby was always able to see its surroundings.

SUMMER SANDALS
In summer, most Basin peoples went barefoot, but some tribes made sandals from coarsely woven tree bark. Sometimes the Southern Paiute made buckskin moccasins, or wove sandals from yucca fiber. These were made according to a traditional design of the Kaibab band of the Southern Paiute.

Californian hunter-gatherers

NATIVE AMERICANS found California as attractive in the 1760s as their American successors did in the 1960s. The reasons were simple. Except for the southeastern desert, the climate and resources made life easy. Warfare was rare and farming almost unknown, the people preferring to be hunter-gatherers. Isolated by deserts and mountains from the warlike tribes to the east, the 50 tribes lived on fish and game, but seeds (especially acorns) played a major role in their diet. Their ceremonies petitioned the spirit world to ensure food and health. The arrival in 1769 of the Spanish, establishing missions in the south, began the erosion of this way of life, and the Gold Rush of 1849 in the north destroyed it.

Map of North America showing the California region

FEATHER BUNCH
The Maidu, nicknamed "Digger Indians" by the Europeans (because they searched for edible roots to supplement their acorn diet), lived in partly underground dwellings, up to 40 ft (12 m) across. At some of their ceremonies, both men and women wore feather bunches (right).

Maidu dance plume, or bunch (worn on crown of head), made of quills, feathers, wood, and string

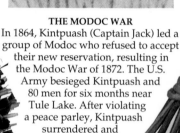

THE MODOC WAR
In 1864, Kintpuash (Captain Jack) led a group of Modoc who refused to accept their new reservation, resulting in the Modoc War of 1872. The U.S. Army besieged Kintpuash and 80 men for six months near Tule Lake. After violating a peace parley, Kintpuash surrendered and was hanged.

Single piece of curved wood forms basic frame of Pomo flail

Elaborate design on ceramic doll echoes tattoo designs on a Mohave warrior

Closely woven netting made of willow

DESERT PEOPLE
The Mohave, typical of the Yuman tribes along the lower Colorado River, farmed the bottom land, relying on the annual flooding of the river for raising crops. By the late 1800s, confined to a reservation, they were selling souvenirs, like these ceramic dolls (above), at a nearby railroad station.

GATHERING SEEDS
The Pomo lived between the ocean and the Coast Range. Their dwellings, each home to several families, were 30-ft (9-m) -long pole frameworks covered with thatch. They were expert hunters and fishermen, but the most important part of their diet was acorns, ground into meal. They also ate seeds, roots, and berries. Women used flails (right) to knock seeds into a collecting, or burden, basket.

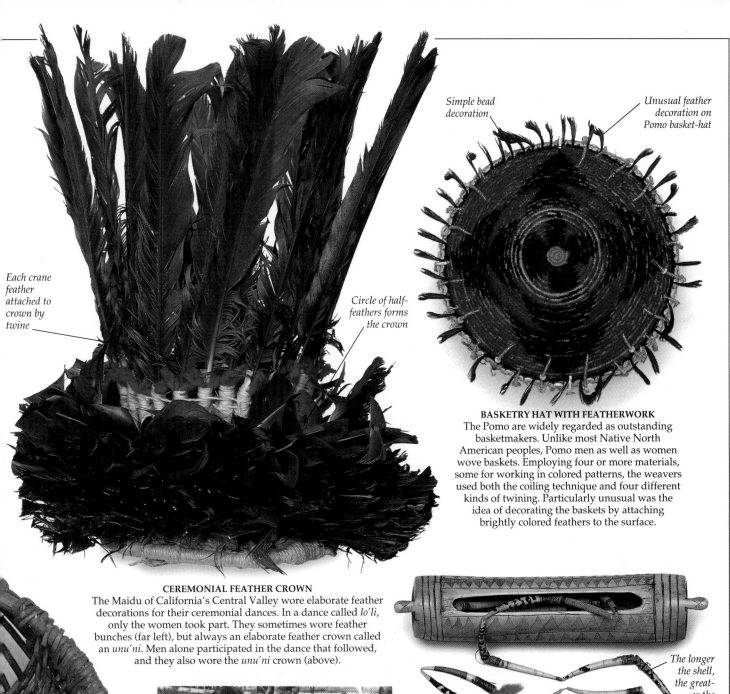

Each crane feather attached to crown by twine

Circle of half-feathers forms the crown

Simple bead decoration

Unusual feather decoration on Pomo basket-hat

BASKETRY HAT WITH FEATHERWORK
The Pomo are widely regarded as outstanding basketmakers. Unlike most Native North American peoples, Pomo men as well as women wove baskets. Employing four or more materials, some for working in colored patterns, the weavers used both the coiling technique and four different kinds of twining. Particularly unusual was the idea of decorating the baskets by attaching brightly colored feathers to the surface.

CEREMONIAL FEATHER CROWN
The Maidu of California's Central Valley wore elaborate feather decorations for their ceremonial dances. In a dance called *lo'li*, only the women took part. They sometimes wore feather bunches (far left), but always an elaborate feather crown called an *unu'ni*. Men alone participated in the dance that followed, and they also wore the *unu'ni* crown (above).

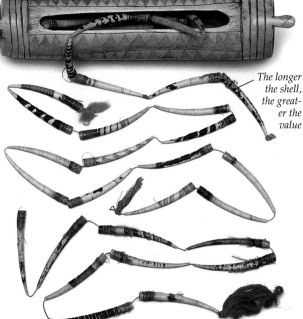

The longer the shell, the greater the value

THE LAST OF THE YAHI
In 1911 the last survivor of the isolated Yahi tribe, long believed to have died out, appeared in a northern California town. He was "adopted" by anthropologists at the University of California, who wished to learn about his way of life. They named him Ishi (Yahi for "man"). Ishi died of tuberculosis in 1916.

SPENDING MONEY
Far to the north, on Vancouver Island, strings of dentalium shells (above) were highly valued ornaments. Brought south by traders of the Tolowa tribe, they were used as a form of money by many of the California peoples. But the Pomo preferred to make a rival currency from the white mineral magnesite, or from clamshells. Most Northern tribes made purses from elk antlers (top), which were strikingly decorated.

The stunning Southwest

THE SOUTHWEST IS A LAND of great majesty and spectacular contrasts, of mountain and desert, scorching heat in summer and cold in winter. Its peoples can trace their ancestry back 2,000 years, and some of their stone and clay villages have been continuously occupied for more than 1,000 years. In this arid land, the Pueblo peoples learned to irrigate their crops with the little water available. Their rituals were closely connected with persuading the beings of the spirit world to bring rain. So, too, were those of the Papago of the desert to the south. Though not warriors, Pueblos sometimes fought each other and defended themselves against Navajo and Apache.

Map of North America showing the Southwest region

Typical geometric decoration

Bird-animal design on coiled basketry Havasupai bowl

Painted wood Zuni lightning symbol set up on a kiva altar

PRAYING FOR RAIN
Both Zuni and Hopi Pueblo peoples lived bounded by rituals that connected them to the spirit world. Every August the Hopi held a nine-day Snake Ceremonial to bring the rain that ensured a good harvest. Snake sticks (symbols of the lightning that comes with rain) were set up on a kiva altar. At the ritual's end, painted dancers held live snakes in their mouths, then released them into the desert.

PEACEFUL LIFE IN AN ISOLATED CANYON
For nearly 900 years the Havasupai have farmed Cataract Canyon in Arizona, using skills learned from the Hopi and irrigating with water from the Colorado River. Isolated in the canyon, they have no tradition of warfare.

PAPAGO POTS
Like their cousins the Pima, the Papago were descended from the Hohokam people, who lived more than 2,000 years ago in settled villages along what is now Arizona's border with Mexico. In tribal life, men were responsible for raising the usual crops of squash, corn, and beans while women wove baskets and made pots.

Unusual effigy of a tattooed woman shapes this Papago pottery vessel

Desert frog was inspiration for bowl's decoration

Traditional black geometric design on a light background

ANCIENT ART
The Pueblo tradition of pottery making stretches back to their ancient ancestors in the region. Styles in design vary among the Pueblos but are always highly decorated in traditional colors of red, black, and white, with geometric or representational designs.

Four step-shaped corners, modeled after frogs, decorate this large, elaborate Zuni bowl, which once belonged to a rain priest

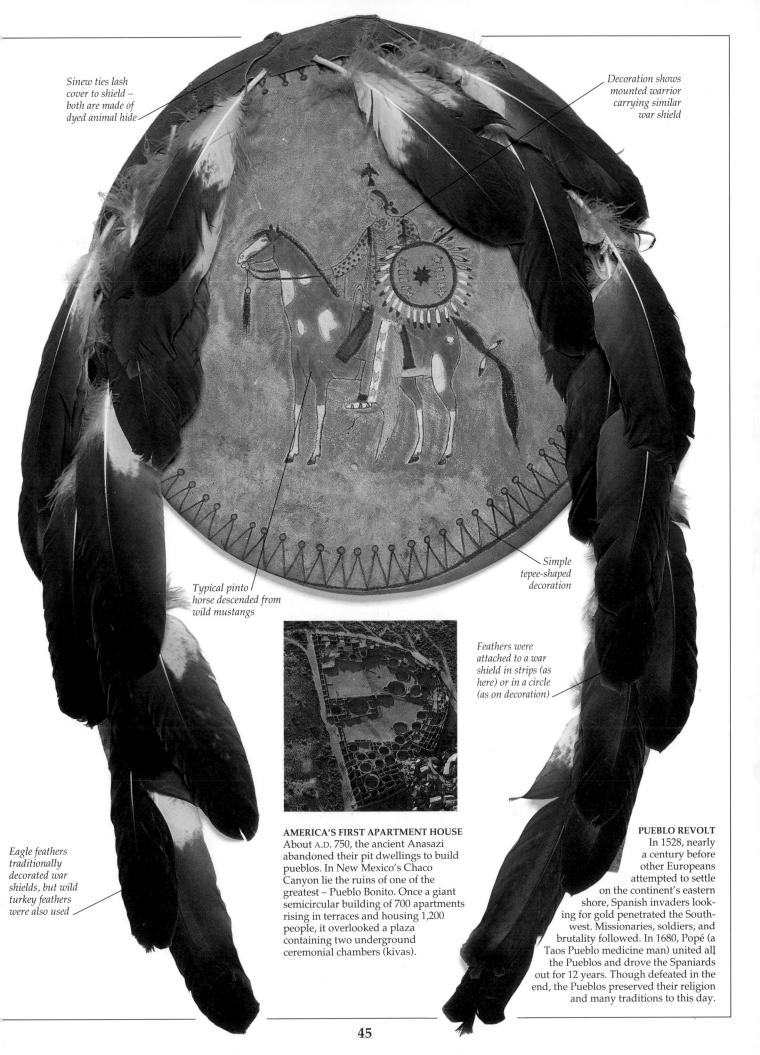

Sinew ties lash cover to shield – both are made of dyed animal hide

Decoration shows mounted warrior carrying similar war shield

Typical pinto horse descended from wild mustangs

Simple tepee-shaped decoration

Feathers were attached to a war shield in strips (as here) or in a circle (as on decoration)

Eagle feathers traditionally decorated war shields, but wild turkey feathers were also used

AMERICA'S FIRST APARTMENT HOUSE
About A.D. 750, the ancient Anasazi abandoned their pit dwellings to build pueblos. In New Mexico's Chaco Canyon lie the ruins of one of the greatest – Pueblo Bonito. Once a giant semicircular building of 700 apartments rising in terraces and housing 1,200 people, it overlooked a plaza containing two underground ceremonial chambers (kivas).

PUEBLO REVOLT
In 1528, nearly a century before other Europeans attempted to settle on the continent's eastern shore, Spanish invaders looking for gold penetrated the Southwest. Missionaries, soldiers, and brutality followed. In 1680, Popé (a Taos Pueblo medicine man) united all the Pueblos and drove the Spaniards out for 12 years. Though defeated in the end, the Pueblos preserved their religion and many traditions to this day.

The Pueblo peoples

ON THE WINDSWEPT TABLETOP ROCKS towering above the desert and along the Southwest's few rivers stand stone and adobe settlements. Today Native Americans inhabit some 30 villages from the Rio Grande to northern Arizona. The first Spanish explorers called the inhabitants Pueblo (village) people, but they were not a single tribe. The villages were independent and the people (including Hopi and Zuni) spoke different languages. From early times they have raised crops of squash, beans, and corn. Their lives are guided by kachinas, spirit beings who enter the bodies of selected men wearing masks and performing sacred dances. Men also govern the community, but women own all property which is inherited by their daughters.

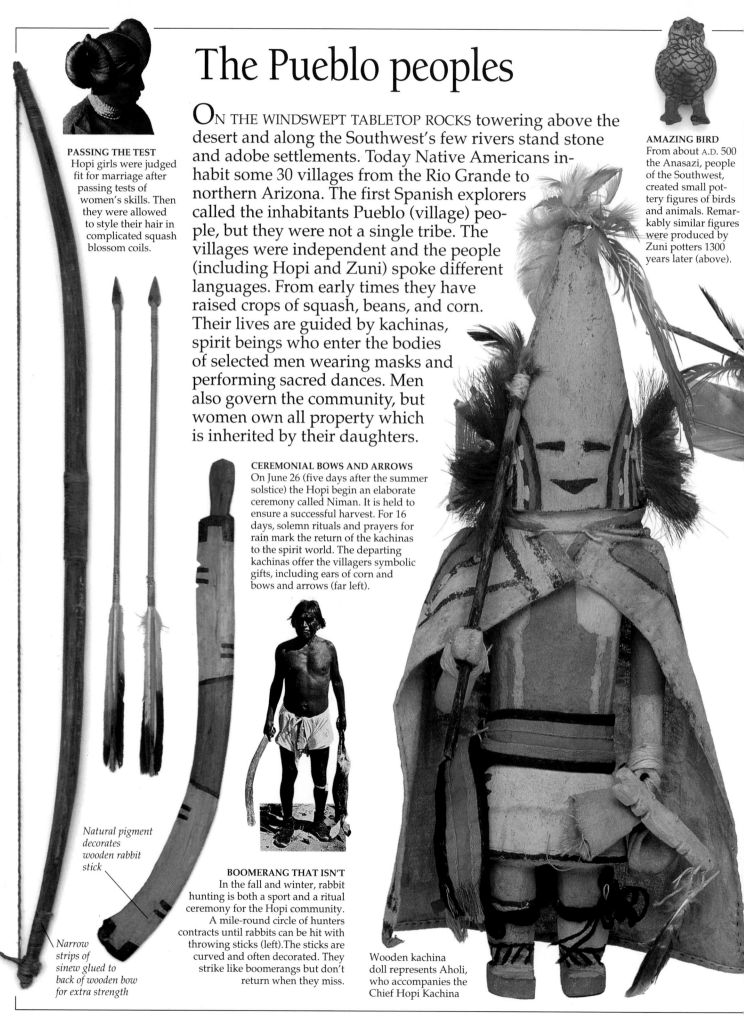

PASSING THE TEST
Hopi girls were judged fit for marriage after passing tests of women's skills. Then they were allowed to style their hair in complicated squash blossom coils.

AMAZING BIRD
From about A.D. 500 the Anasazi, people of the Southwest, created small pottery figures of birds and animals. Remarkably similar figures were produced by Zuni potters 1300 years later (above).

CEREMONIAL BOWS AND ARROWS
On June 26 (five days after the summer solstice) the Hopi begin an elaborate ceremony called Niman. It is held to ensure a successful harvest. For 16 days, solemn rituals and prayers for rain mark the return of the kachinas to the spirit world. The departing kachinas offer the villagers symbolic gifts, including ears of corn and bows and arrows (far left).

Natural pigment decorates wooden rabbit stick

Narrow strips of sinew glued to back of wooden bow for extra strength

BOOMERANG THAT ISN'T
In the fall and winter, rabbit hunting is both a sport and a ritual ceremony for the Hopi community. A mile-round circle of hunters contracts until rabbits can be hit with throwing sticks (left). The sticks are curved and often decorated. They strike like boomerangs but don't return when they miss.

Wooden kachina doll represents Aholi, who accompanies the Chief Hopi Kachina

Feathers typically decorate heads of kachina dolls

Maria Martinez's matte-black-on-polished-black pots have become famous this century

Feather from a bird of prey

FAMOUS POTTERY
For 900 years Pueblo peoples have developed a highly individual style of decorated pottery. San Ildefonso Pueblo traditionally produced geometric designs in two colors. Here, in 1919, Julian Martinez invented a matte-black-on-polished-black design for pots made by his wife, Maria.

Horns and other animal forms sometimes appeared on masks of kachina dolls, and on masks of kachina dancers

Kachina doll given as gift from kachina dancer who pretends to threaten a child and demands food – if appeased, the child is unharmed

Nakachok, a painted wooden Hopi kachina doll

NOT A TOY
Kachina dolls were not toys but a vital part of the education of every Pueblo child. These dolls, specially carved to represent the different types of kachina, taught children about the appearance and roles of the many kachinas. Kachina-doll carving was most highly developed by the Hopi and Zuni.

Nataska, a Hopi kachina doll, helps discipline erring children

Apache and Navajo

THE ARID MOUNTAINS and deserts of the Southwest became home to the Apache and Navajo, who may have migrated south from the far Northwest in the 1400s. Hunters and warriors, they raided first their Pueblo neighbors and later the colonizing Spanish pushing north from Mexico. From both they learned important agricultural skills. The Navajo combined sheep raising, farming, and raiding until local American forces under Kit Carson (1809–68) forced their surrender in 1864. Rebuilding their way of life, they added silverwork to their arts. Some Apache, learning from the Pueblo villagers, took up farming, but most remained hunter-raiders. Feared by other tribes and by Europeans as the fiercest warriors in the Southwest, they faced their final defeat in the mid-1880s.

BEJEWELED
Famous for their beautiful jewelry, the Navajo decorated this leather wrist guard in their typical style, with silver and turquoise.

BRAVE WARRIOR
Geronimo (1829–1909) was his Mexican name; his Apache name (Goyanthlay) meant "the Yawner." He became the most famous Apache warrior and fought the American invasion of Apache lands in the 1860s and 1870s. He was caught in 1877 and confined on the San Carlos reservation in Arizona. On his escape in 1881, he resumed raiding – to the terror of both Mexican and American settlers. He was photographed (above, far right) just before he finally surrendered in 1886.

BEST FOOT FORWARD
As an alternative to wearing moccasins with separate hide leggings to protect their legs from thornbrush, Apaches wore a one-piece soft boot, or "long moccasin," made from antelope skin or deerskin. Usually, men's long moccasins reached to just below the knee, while those of women extended above it.

Head of stone on Apache war club

Delicately colored beadwork decoration

Hide tie for fastening child's long moccasin below the knee

Fine beadwork decoration

Metal stud decoration

Wooden shaft covered in rawhide for a firm grip

Navajo whip made from dyed horsehair

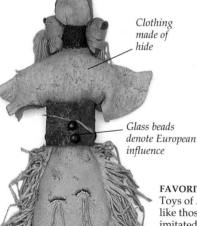

Clothing made of hide

Glass beads denote European influence

FAVORITE DOLL
Toys of Apache children, like those of children everywhere, imitated the adult world into which they would grow. This rag doll has its hair arranged in the Hopi style worn by an unmarried girl. When an Apache girl entered puberty, a four-day ceremony was held. Ritual singing alternated with feasting. Like the Hopi girls, an Apache girl was taught her future responsibilities by an older woman and ran a ritual race to prove her strength and courage. After this, she was ready for marriage.

INTO BATTLE!
Like all Native Americans, the Navajo and Apache knew nothing of horses until they met Spanish colonists with their mounts in the 1500s. However, they quickly learned to use and breed them, especially for warfare. The Navajo whip (far right) is very similar to the quirt (from the Spanish *cuerta*) used by American cowboys and Mexican *vaqueros*. The Apache war club was a good close-quarter weapon – the decoration on this example (near right) is particularly handsome.

Upper bar

Shed rod

Colored wool yarn

Wood batten separates upright threads

Comb beats cross-threads into place

Motifs evolved since the 1870s, including diamond shapes

A TRADITIONAL WEAVE
Navajo beliefs tell how Spider Woman (one of their Holy People and a spirit being) first taught women how to weave. Skills are passed down from mother to daughter in a tradition that has lasted for generations. Tools were often handed on, like the batten to separate the warp (up-thread) and the comb to beat in place the weft (cross-thread). All property in Navajo clans passed from mother to daughter.

Beaded Apache tobacco pouch fringed with metal decoration

Tassel decoration made of hide

Wool attaches woven rug to lower bar

BEAUTIFULLY WOVEN
The Navajo first learned weaving skills in the late 1600s from the Pueblo peoples, using wool from sheep originally raided from the Spanish. By the mid-1800s, Navajo textiles were traded all over the West. Blankets were woven in intricate patterns and traditional colors, which changed over time. From the late 1800s, American merchants encouraged the weaving of rugs with pictorial designs, like the one above. This form of Navajo art is now well known and valued worldwide.

Cow's-tail attachment, dyed red

FINE BEADWORK
The Apache did not become known for pottery like the Hopi, nor for weaving and silverwork like the Navajo. Apache women, however, made beautiful baskets of willow rods and did fine beadwork, as shown in this elaborate tobacco pouch.

Papago and Pima

IN THE PARCHED DESERTS of what is now Arizona and northern Mexico, over 2,000 years ago the Hohokam people built irrigation systems to raise crops. Their descendants are the Pima and Papago (the Papagos' name for themselves, O'Odham, means "the People"). Using this inherited knowledge of river irrigation, the Pima settled in villages by the Salt and Gila rivers, raising corn, squash, and beans, and adding wheat around 1700. Their surplus of food became so large, they supplied California miners and, during the Civil War, the Union Army. The desert-dwelling Papago had to rely on seasonal flood water for farming and so stayed seminomadic. From the fermented fruit of the saguaro cactus they made wine to be used in rituals. Both tribes had similar ceremonies and both worshiped two main divine beings – Elder Brother and Earthmaker.

Traditional horned toad on Pima basket

ENDLESS USES
As nearly unbreakable containers, baskets had endless uses. Bowl-shaped ones were used for storing corn and shallow ones for carrying fruit collected from the top of the saguaro cactus. Designs picturing animals began to emerge in the 1800s.

Feather-decorated hide covers this Papago wooden shield

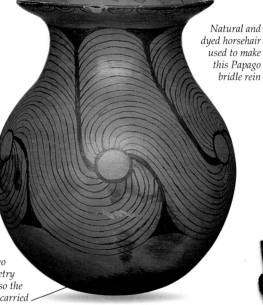

THE ART OF BASKETMAKING
Basketmaking became an art among the Pima. Traditional techniques involved close coils of willow wound around bulrushes. Patterns were produced by adding pieces of the black devil's claw plant to make a striking contrast. Papago basketry also borrowed from Spanish designs. A basket was sometimes so large that the maker had to climb inside to finish it!

BRIDLE WEAR
The Papago were seminomadic, with few water resources. Horses were useful for traveling between their summer field villages in the desert and their winter well villages near mountain springs.

MOCK BATTLES
Papago and Pima ceremonies included mock battles in which shields like this one were used. Though not fierce raiders like the Apache, they found war with other tribes was often unavoidable and were effective and successful warriors. In the Civil War, the Pima defended Arizona on behalf of the Union, defeating Confederate forces. After 1865 they served as valued scouts for the army in its campaigns against the Apache.

SIMPLE BUT EXQUISITE
Like the other peoples of the Southwest, the Pima and Papago were potters. Compared with the Hopi and Zuni, however, their designs were much simpler.

Rounded bottom of this Papago pottery water jar fits into a basketry ring worn on top of the head, so the jar could be easily carried

Natural and dyed horsehair used to make this Papago bridle rein

Feathers from a bird of prey

Massed eagle feathers decorate top (and back) of clown mask

Solid thread construction marks hole for eye

Papago clown mask seen from front

Rear view of Papago clown mask

Flap, attached to crown, hangs down the back

SACRED CROP CEREMONY
Pima and Papago ceremonies centered on the single most important thing in their lives, the successful raising of their crops in an arid land. In each village one man, named the Keeper of the Smoke, was in charge of the ceremonies. Every fourth year both tribes held a special celebration (called the Viikita) for the harvest. Ritual dancers, costumed and masked as sacred clowns, acted out the people's dependence on the land, the weather, and the divine beings.

RAIN SPIRITS
Because they lived in the desert, the Papago had ceremonies to bring rain. They made special journeys to where they believed the rain spirits dwelt to beg them to return to the tribal lands. Every summer the Papago performed a ritual in which they drank huge quantities of cactus wine, believing that an alcoholic stupor drove out evil and pleased the rain spirits.

Black design on front of canvas hood (made from a flour bag) symbolizes a rain cloud

Horsehair braid decorated with red cloth

Land of the totem poles

Raven above a bear

Abalone-inlaid ivory handle

BETWEEN THE DARK FORESTS and the ocean's edge in the rainy Northwest, there grew an extraordinary culture almost untouched by Europeans until the late 1700s. The people of this area, divided into about 30 tribes, never developed agriculture, but were able to live comfortably from the teeming riches of the sea, the forest, and the rivers that filled with salmon during their annual runs. The bountiful environment allowed development of a splendid art and a complex society of nobles, commoners, and slaves.

Map of North America showing the Northwest region

Wealthy families, proud of their status, expressed it in sumptuous ceremonies and monumental artworks, especially the towering wood totem poles.

Hide strap used to lash knife to wrist

Elegantly carved fins on Haida halibut club

Carving on the upper part of this Haida totem pole represents a raven

HOOKED ON HALIBUT
The island-dwelling Haida relied on fishing. Halibut were caught by setting hooks close to the ocean bed. Once hauled to the surface, such fish had to be stunned with clubs immediately – at up to 400 lb (180 kg), their struggles might upset the canoe. The canoe was dug out of the trunk of a giant cedar and its prow decorated with an elaborate abstract carving.

Iron blade of Tlingit fighting knife

WAR PARTIES
Northwest Coast warfare was typically a quick raid, either for revenge or to acquire plunder and slaves. The northernmost tribes also waged wars to drive away neighboring enemy tribes and control their land. Warriors wore wooden helmets and body armor made from strips of wood joined with rawhide. Weapons were bows, clubs, and knives (above). War knives originally had blades of stone or bone, later of traded iron. Knives were lashed to the wrist during battle.

Intricate carving adorns this model of a Haida tomb

PERIOD OF MOURNING
A dead Haida was mourned ceremonially at home for a period of four to six days. The body was then placed in a grave box and taken out of the house through a specially made exit. The remains were put in a grave house, perhaps as large as an ordinary home, and commemorated with a memorial post.

TOTEM POLE VILLAGE
Architecture was one of the great achievements of the Northwest Coast peoples. The huge wooden houses had walls of cedar planks fitted over a massive cedar framework. They were designed by architects who supervised skilled artisans and gangs of laborers, often slaves from other tribes. Several related families lived in a house. Living space reflected rank, the highest place of honor being the back wall. A forest of totem poles dotted the village. Some were built into the fronts of houses, with holes at their bases for door openings. Free-standing poles were often memorials.

Small frog carving

A FAMILY'S STATUS

Totem poles were not idols, as Christian missionaries believed, but monuments proclaiming a family's status by recording its family tree. Every household claimed through its legends a relationship with a spirit being in the form of a noble animal such as a raven, wolf, bear, or eagle. Carvings representing these beings were family crests, much like coats of arms in medieval Europe.

Totem pole carved from trunk of a cedar tree

Lower carvings on totem pole depict marriage alliances or other important family events

This pole is 20 ft (6 m) long, but a whole totem pole stands more than 40 ft (12 m) high

SMOKING PIPES

Tlingit men never smoked until they obtained tobacco from white traders, c. 1800. Then they began to produce an astonishing variety of intricately carved wooden pipes with metal bowls, used only by men – women did not smoke. Designs depicted crests. This Tlingit pipe has two carved and painted wooden wolves and is inlaid with abalone shells.

Horned owl carved on top third of totem pole

Head of bird of prey

Represents feathers of a bird

Small Haida totem pole or grave post

SECRETS BEHIND TOTEM POLES

Wealthy families commissioned sculptors to carve totem poles for various purposes, mostly related to burial rites and memorials to the dead. The heir of a deceased chief might erect a pole in the chief's honor as part of the process of taking over his role and titles. Sometimes a dead chief's remains were interred in a box on top of the pole. Raising a totem pole was always accompanied by a great ceremony: the potlatch (pp. 56–57).

Art second to none

IN THE FLICKERING FIRELIGHT of a Northwest house during the winter ceremonies, two great arts were dramatically displayed together – ritual dances and intricately carved masks. The dances, held by secret societies to initiate a new member, enacted the links between ancestors and spirit beings. Masked dancers represented the power and continuing presence of the spirit world. The ceremony was both ritual and theater, for the dancers used spectacular special effects to enhance the story they were telling. Membership in a society, the right to dance, and the possession of masks helped define privileges in this status-conscious culture. Both male and female shamans also wore ritual masks in their role as doctors.

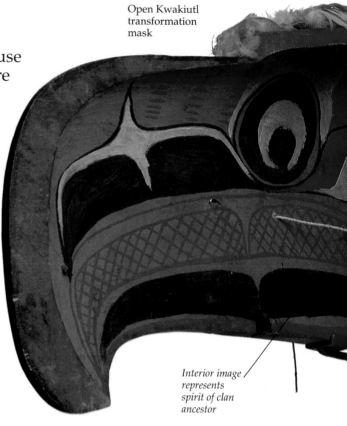

Open Kwakiutl transformation mask

Interior image represents spirit of clan ancestor

Cord, looping through eye and cheekbones, is pulled to open up the mask

Haida wooden rattle in form of a hawk

Bar supplies leverage to pull open the beak

When closed, this Kwakiutl transformation mask looks like an eagle's head

Abalone shell forms the bird's eye

SHAMAN'S RATTLES
Shamans were revered by the tribe for their awesome powers. These derived from special access to the spirit world through a personal guardian spirit, summoned by singing and the shaking of a sacred rattle. Illness was thought to be caused by the intrusion of a small object into the body or by the loss or theft of the soul by spirits, often manipulated by witches. In a dramatic ceremony performed for a fee, a shaman cured the sick person by removing the object or by restoring the lost soul. The witch was then identified and punished.

Three witches planning evil activities are guarded by an octopus (near handle)

Dead man with protruding tongue in bill of kingfisher

Red ball is the Sun, once stolen; raven is now releasing it to light up the world

SECRET SOCIETIES
The Kwakiutl, who probably began the secret societies that eventually spread across the Northwest, had three: the Shaman Society, representing violent and threatening spirits; the Dluwulaxa, linked to the sky spirits; and the Nutlam, whose ancestor was the wolf spirit. Most important to the Shaman Society was a cannibal spirit – the dancers in this ceremony, called Hamatsa, had great prestige and wore particularly elaborate masks. Starting in mid-November the Kwakiutls held Winter Rituals for four months to establish a connection between uninitiated youths and a particular supernatural being, after which the youths became members of the appropriate secret society.

Tlingit shaman's wooden oyster catcher rattle

Tlingit wooden raven rattle

Spirit represented in quasi-human form

Painting inside bird's head shows internal view of eye, nostril, and beak

BEHIND THE MASK
Separate from the winter ceremonies were dances that displayed the household's privileges. This spectacular Kwakiutl transformation mask (changing from a bird's face to a human one) was probably part of such a dance. It was fixed to the dancer's head by a frame of wickerwork and animal sinews. The two bars at the back were linked by draw cords to the sides of the beak, and a third cord led to the lower part of the beak. Manipulating the cords instantly transformed an eagle spirit into one with a fierce human face.

Head has human features except for hooked beak rather than a nose

Bella Coola Sun Mask

Four oval faces, each flanked by a pair of upraised hands, surround the Sun

Carved, painted spherical face represents the Sun

RED AS THE SUN
The Bella Coola lived in northern British Columbia, Canada, between two groups of the Kwakiutl. Membership in their Dance Society, usually hereditary, was a coveted privilege because it brought great status. At their four-night winter ceremony, members performed dances taught to them by the spirit beings of the sky. Wearing spherical masks, such as the Spirit of the Sun (at right), the dancers acted out with great drama the central stories of the tribe's beliefs. Masks were designed for a striking effect rather than a readily identifiable spirit.

The power of potlatch

In THE NORTHWEST, gaining wealth brought the possibility of status, but in the great potlatch ceremonies, giving wealth away guaranteed it. Potlatches were lavish distributions of gifts from host to guests, who might number in the hundreds. They took place in order to gain acceptance for a change in status or the acquisition of privileges. Potlatches did not bankrupt the giver. Being host at one potlatch guaranteed being a guest – and therefore a receiver of gifts – at others. In a society of often intense rivalries, potlatches siphoned off the tensions that otherwise might have led to war. Potlatches are still held today. A Canadian government ban, from 1884 to 1951, was defied by the Kwakiutl, and there has been a general revival of the ceremony since the 1960s.

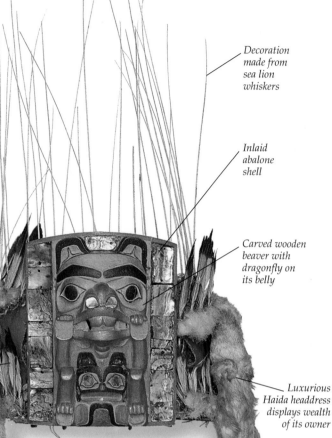

Decoration made from sea lion whiskers

Inlaid abalone shell

Carved wooden beaver with dragonfly on its belly

Flicker feather

Luxurious Haida headdress displays wealth of its owner

Ermine pelt

HAIDA HEADDRESS
Much of the artistic activity among Northwest Coast tribes went into creating their magnificent potlatch costumes. In the 1800s the Haida copied headdresses for ceremonial dances from more northern tribes. Such a headdress (above) would have been worn in association with a Chilkat blanket (below).

Image of family crest engraved on this 3-ft-high (1-m) Haida copper

MOST PRECIOUS POSSESSION
Shield-shaped plaques of engraved metal, called coppers, were immensely valuable and highly prized as potlatch gifts. Although coppers as symbols of wealth were invented by the Northwest Coast tribes before the arrival of the Europeans, they became even more popular during the 19th-century fur trade period because of the tribes' easy access to copper.

Chief Tutlidi and son at Fort Rupert in 1894

BESTOWING A COPPER
The gift of a copper demonstrated great wealth and thus earned prestige, honoring both giver and receiver. Alternatively, in a flamboyant gesture a chief might deliberately break a copper; shown at left is a chief giving away a copper in honor of his son and heir. Rivalry between chiefs was often intense, so one might break a copper and give the pieces to his rival. To avoid shame the recipient was instantly expected to break a copper of equal or greater value.

DRESSED FOR A POTLATCH
Chilkat blankets and dancing dresses (right) were highly valued. They were woven from mountain goat's wool and cedar bark by Tlingit women. The weavers were paid a high fee, so possession of such objects showed the owner's wealth. The dresses were passed on to relatives and were ostentatiously displayed at potlatches, where a host honored his guests by giving them pieces cut from his dress.

Every ring section denotes that the wearer had hosted one potlatch

Symbolic crest design, provided by the men, who painted it onto a board for the women weavers

A CEREMONIAL HAT
Potlatches were held to celebrate the marriage of a chief, to inaugurate a new clan house, or to mark the death of an old chief. The chief of a household was responsible for managing its harvest from sea and forest (from which he took a share) and for managing relations with other households. At potlatches a host, wearing ceremonial hat (left) and costume, had help from a speaker, who made the formal announcements, and from a master of ceremonies, who also invited the many guests.

Ermine pelt decoration

WHAT A FEAST!
Potlatches were accompanied by a spectacular feast that might last up to 12 days. The host tried to provide more food than could be eaten by his guests. They paid respect by eating until they were sick. Food included seal meat, fish, berries, and vegetables served with fish oil in feast dishes like this large bear-shaped vessel.

Tlingit bear-shaped wooden bowl with shell inlays

Stylized bear carved into Tlingit feast dish

A WORK OF ART
Feast dishes were elaborately carved works of art, part of the visible symbols of a household's rank and wealth. The largest, which could be the size (and shape) of a small canoe, were placed in front of the guest chiefs, who ate from them using spoons of mountain goat horn or wood. Ordinary guests had their food ladled into smaller dishes (above).

Thin strands of spruce roots used in making this Tlingit basketry hat

Painting of crow depicts a family crest

Hat would have been made in rainy weather to prevent materials from drying out

Northern hunters

Map of North America showing the Subarctic region

LIFE IN THE SUBARCTIC demanded extraordinary ingenuity, courage, and self-reliance. Summers were short and winters ferocious in the far northern forests and on the tundra. In this hard land, the search for food dominated life. All 30 Subarctic tribes survived by hunting and fishing, adapting to a nomadic life. The Chipewyan depended on caribou and followed the great herds on their seasonal migrations. The Ojibwa were forest hunters, moving between summer and winter camps. The Naskapi of the taiga (coniferous forests) relied on caribou and all kinds of game, like moose and beaver. Meat and fish were preserved by sun-drying or smoking. Hallmarks of the region were wigwams, snowshoes, the birchbark canoe, and skin clothing.

Hood on Ojibwa child's winter coat protects face from severe cold and wind

Hide fastening

Strips of rabbit skin woven together

A CHARMED HEAD
Though hunted, bears were regarded with awe by the Subarctic peoples, who believed they possessed powerful spirits. Skulls were thought to retain the bear's spirit and were kept as charms. A hunter would always pray to apologize to a bear's spirit, explaining his need for food and to ask for future successful hunts.

Simple decoration on skull denoted a special honor to bear's spirit

WARM WINTER WRAP
Winter clothing, generally made of tanned caribou skins with hair side inward, consisted of coats, mittens, leggings or trousers, moccasins, and hoods. Children sometimes wore winter coats woven from strips of rabbit skin. There were big differences between Eastern and Western tribes in styles of decoration. For example, Easterners painted unique red designs on their coats, while Far Westerners used porcupine quills, shells, and beads.

Beaded decoration shows European influence

Strap made of plaited yarn

Slavey tobacco pouch

Sharp end of caribou bone for scraping away flesh

A BEAR-FUR BAG
Spirits (both good and evil) were soothed through prayers and offerings of tobacco, the smoke rising to comfort the spirits. Tobacco was important in religious and ceremonial life. It was often presented as an invitation to a ceremony or feast, and a gift of tobacco was accepted by the recipient as a great honor.

SKIN DRESSING
Preparing caribou skins was a woman's job, and a long and messy one. Split caribou bones, like this Chipewyan set, were used to remove the hair, if not needed, and to scrape away bits of flesh. Next a soup of rotting caribou brains was rubbed into the skin for a smelly but effective tanning process. After a washing, the skin was stretched on a frame and dried, then pulled and worked by hand until pliable. Last, it was smoked over a fire for a final curing.

Naskapi adult's snowshoe

Netting lashed to frame

MOOSE HUNTING
In this detail of a George Catlin painting the hunter is on snowshoes and is holding a spear. He is gliding easily across a snowdrift in pursuit of a moose. A windy day deadened the sound of the snowshoes, while bright sunlight helped harden the animals' footprints in the snow, making it easier to track them.

Netting was separated by using wooden or bone needles

Rawhide netting often made of moose skin

Hide thongs for tying snowshoe to foot

MAKING A SNOWSHOE
Snowshoe frames were made from a long piece of birch softened and bent with steam, then dried and seasoned. Next, crossbars were slotted into the frame. The netting (called babiche) was cut in continuous strips from rawhide. Shapes developed to meet different sorts of terrain and types of snow. In the Far North, shoes were long and narrow; in the East they were oval or round – as shown in this Cree child's snowshoe.

Birch frame

IN DEEP SNOW
Snowshoes allowed the Subarctic peoples to extend their hunting and seasonal migrations into areas otherwise made impassable by deep snow. Moose hunting in winter depended on snowshoes. The hunter could easily follow a moose by its tracks and glide swiftly across the surface of snowdrifts that bogged the moose down.

TRANSPORT BY TOBOGGAN
For transporting goods over snow, toboggans eased the strain on a person's back. Subarctic toboggans were usually made of split-log boards, steam-curled at the front to ride over the snow. They varied in length; some were as long as 8 ft (2.5 m). Toboggans were usually hauled by men, though some tribes, like the Ojibwa, used dogs. The Naskapi despised their long-time enemies, the Inuit, for using dogsleds.

Model of Naskapi man of eastern Canada hauling a toboggan

SUMMER ENCAMPMENT ON CANADA'S LAKE HURON
Canadian artist Paul Kane (1810–71) painted an impression of an Ojibwa summer camp (detail above) in the mid-1800s. The Ojibwa left their winter camps in late March to spend the summer fishing, berry picking, harvesting wild rice, and living in birchbark wigwams.

The frozen Arctic

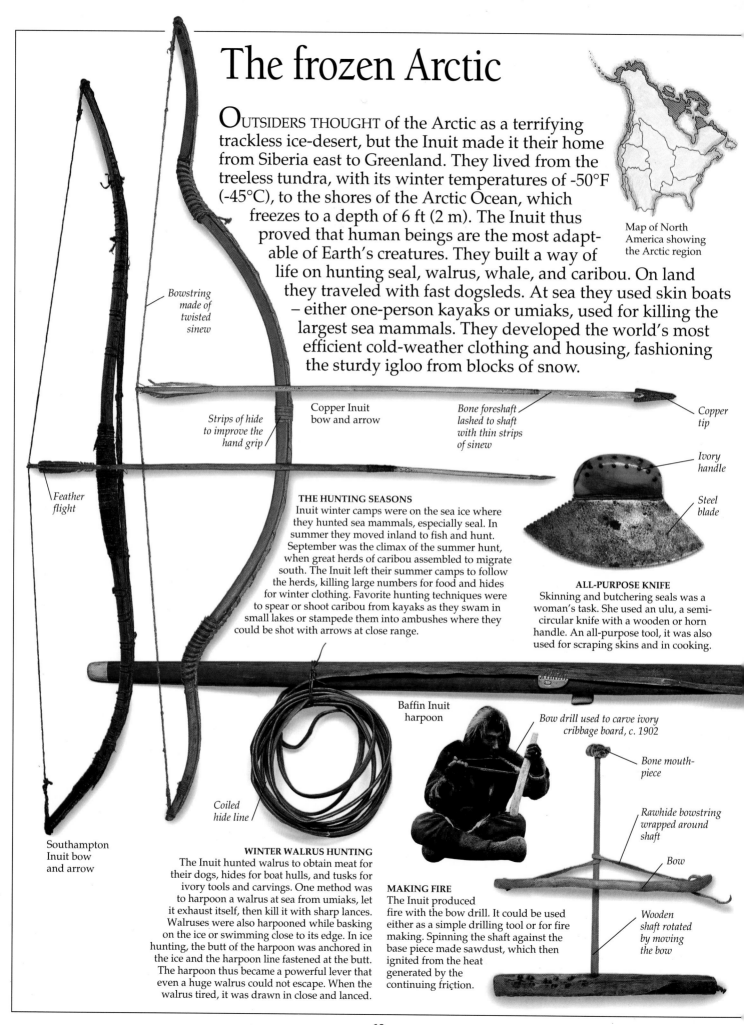

OUTSIDERS THOUGHT of the Arctic as a terrifying trackless ice-desert, but the Inuit made it their home from Siberia east to Greenland. They lived from the treeless tundra, with its winter temperatures of -50°F (-45°C), to the shores of the Arctic Ocean, which freezes to a depth of 6 ft (2 m). The Inuit thus proved that human beings are the most adaptable of Earth's creatures. They built a way of life on hunting seal, walrus, whale, and caribou. On land they traveled with fast dogsleds. At sea they used skin boats – either one-person kayaks or umiaks, used for killing the largest sea mammals. They developed the world's most efficient cold-weather clothing and housing, fashioning the sturdy igloo from blocks of snow.

Map of North America showing the Arctic region

Bowstring made of twisted sinew

Strips of hide to improve the hand grip

Copper Inuit bow and arrow

Bone foreshaft lashed to shaft with thin strips of sinew

Copper tip

Feather flight

Ivory handle

Steel blade

THE HUNTING SEASONS
Inuit winter camps were on the sea ice where they hunted sea mammals, especially seal. In summer they moved inland to fish and hunt. September was the climax of the summer hunt, when great herds of caribou assembled to migrate south. The Inuit left their summer camps to follow the herds, killing large numbers for food and hides for winter clothing. Favorite hunting techniques were to spear or shoot caribou from kayaks as they swam in small lakes or stampede them into ambushes where they could be shot with arrows at close range.

ALL-PURPOSE KNIFE
Skinning and butchering seals was a woman's task. She used an ulu, a semi-circular knife with a wooden or horn handle. An all-purpose tool, it was also used for scraping skins and in cooking.

Baffin Inuit harpoon

Bow drill used to carve ivory cribbage board, c. 1902

Bone mouth-piece

Rawhide bowstring wrapped around shaft

Bow

Coiled hide line

Southampton Inuit bow and arrow

WINTER WALRUS HUNTING
The Inuit hunted walrus to obtain meat for their dogs, hides for boat hulls, and tusks for ivory tools and carvings. One method was to harpoon a walrus at sea from umiaks, let it exhaust itself, then kill it with sharp lances. Walruses were also harpooned while basking on the ice or swimming close to its edge. In ice hunting, the butt of the harpoon was anchored in the ice and the harpoon line fastened at the butt. The harpoon thus became a powerful lever that even a huge walrus could not escape. When the walrus tired, it was drawn in close and lanced.

MAKING FIRE
The Inuit produced fire with the bow drill. It could be used either as a simple drilling tool or for fire making. Spinning the shaft against the base piece made sawdust, which then ignited from the heat generated by the continuing friction.

Wooden shaft rotated by moving the bow

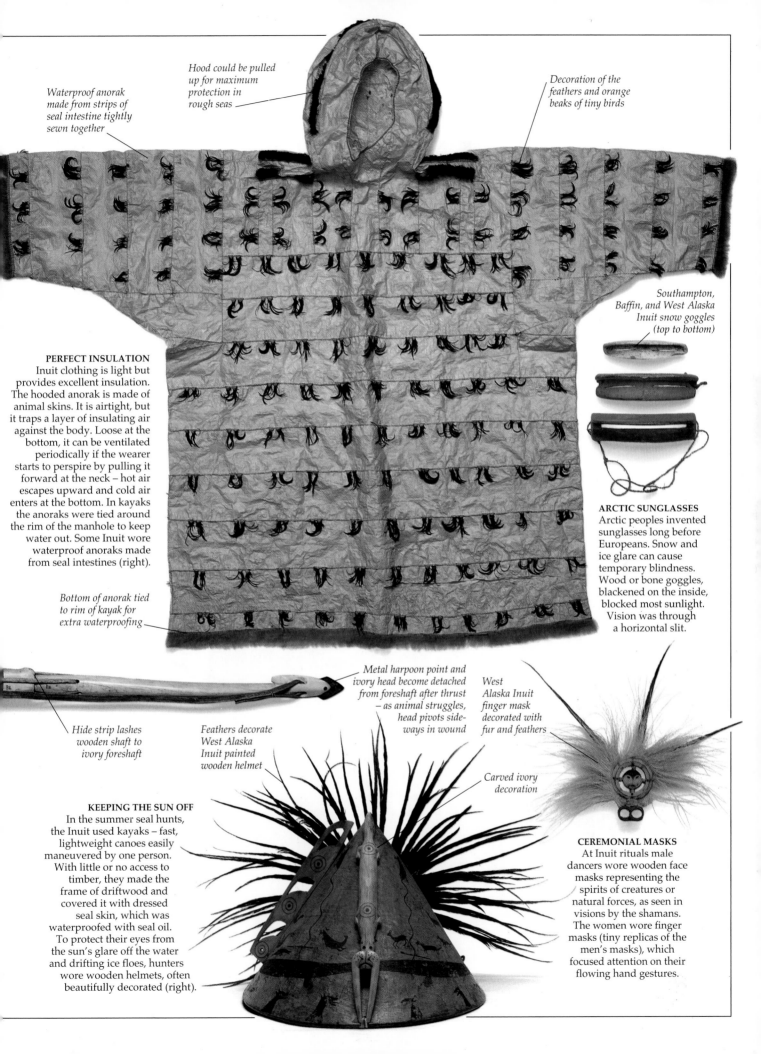

Waterproof anorak made from strips of seal intestine tightly sewn together

Hood could be pulled up for maximum protection in rough seas

Decoration of the feathers and orange beaks of tiny birds

PERFECT INSULATION
Inuit clothing is light but provides excellent insulation. The hooded anorak is made of animal skins. It is airtight, but it traps a layer of insulating air against the body. Loose at the bottom, it can be ventilated periodically if the wearer starts to perspire by pulling it forward at the neck – hot air escapes upward and cold air enters at the bottom. In kayaks the anoraks were tied around the rim of the manhole to keep water out. Some Inuit wore waterproof anoraks made from seal intestines (right).

Bottom of anorak tied to rim of kayak for extra waterproofing

Southampton, Baffin, and West Alaska Inuit snow goggles (top to bottom)

ARCTIC SUNGLASSES
Arctic peoples invented sunglasses long before Europeans. Snow and ice glare can cause temporary blindness. Wood or bone goggles, blackened on the inside, blocked most sunlight. Vision was through a horizontal slit.

Hide strip lashes wooden shaft to ivory foreshaft

Feathers decorate West Alaska Inuit painted wooden helmet

Metal harpoon point and ivory head become detached from foreshaft after thrust – as animal struggles, head pivots sideways in wound

West Alaska Inuit finger mask decorated with fur and feathers

Carved ivory decoration

KEEPING THE SUN OFF
In the summer seal hunts, the Inuit used kayaks – fast, lightweight canoes easily maneuvered by one person. With little or no access to timber, they made the frame of driftwood and covered it with dressed seal skin, which was waterproofed with seal oil. To protect their eyes from the sun's glare off the water and drifting ice floes, hunters wore wooden helmets, often beautifully decorated (right).

CEREMONIAL MASKS
At Inuit rituals male dancers wore wooden face masks representing the spirits of creatures or natural forces, as seen in visions by the shamans. The women wore finger masks (tiny replicas of the men's masks), which focused attention on their flowing hand gestures.

Modern times

THE "VANISHING INDIAN" was how Native North Americans were regarded a century ago. They were expected eventually to join white society or simply die out, but they have refused to do either. Now numbering 2.5 million in the U.S. and Canada, more than half living outside reservations, Native North Americans are reviving tribal traditions and seeking their own role in a multicultural nation. U.S. and Canadian government policy, even when well-meant, tended to make reservations dependent on government support, while tribal resources were plundered by business interests. Despair accompanied unemployment, disease, and lack of education – all far higher than the national average. From the 1970s, militant protests have dramatized key issues but have been less effective than using the law to force compensation for lost rights. Today, many Native peoples hope to bring back traditional forms of decision making and leadership.

Coca-Cola bottle on a pedestal

Modern interpretation of traditional Mohawk hairstyle

Mohawk spirit motif

WALKING HIGH STEEL
Mohawks of the Northeast are famous for their dangerous and highly skilled work in erecting bridges and skyscrapers. An original twelve, hired in 1886, taught relatives and friends how to "walk the high steel." The 1930s New York skyscraper boom created a Mohawk community that continues to sell its remarkable skills today. Old traditions of bravery and kinship thus operate in a modern industry.

MODERN ART
Native North American identity can today inspire an artist but need not dictate subjects. Former high-steel worker Richard Glazer Danay painted this "hard hat" as a modern Mohawk headdress. He mixes sarcastic images of American life, classical art allusions, and motifs echoing Mohawk traditions.

Modern Mohawk "headdress" painted by Native American artist Richard Glazer Danay in 1982

Figure alludes to a Renaissance painting

ANCIENT CEREMONIES
Traditional ceremonies retain force and meaning for the Apache. Dancers (left) wearing symbolic masks, headdresses, and body paint represent Gans (mountain spirit beings). Directed by a shaman, the Gans impersonators perform rituals to gain protection against hostile spirits or to heal the sick. Gans dancers may also provide entertainment at the four-day celebrations marking a girl's coming of age.

Navajo woman baking bread, using traditional oven and equipment

CARRYING ON TRADITIONS
Over 200,000 Navajo live on their 15-million-acre (6-million-ha) reservation, chiefly in Arizona – the largest in the U.S. The Navajo have long been divided over how far to accept white American ways. The tribal council still holds meetings in Navajo, and ceremonies (particularly those for curing illness) remain central to tribal life. Traditional Navajo art, such as weaving and silverwork, is an important source of income.

SOCIAL BENEFITS
Using their rights over their own lands, confirmed by a 1988 Act of Congress, Native Americans have opened gambling casinos in 33 states across the U.S. Casinos provide jobs, and profits pay for housing, schools, and health care. However, arguments over how to spend the money have already divided tribes, and some leaders fear gambling will have bad social effects.

THE POWER OF POWWOW
Though never abandoned, powwows have again become hugely popular. Nearly a thousand were held in 1993, attended by 90 percent of Native North Americans. They are a way of asserting Native peoples' identity. Many tribes participate in these weekend celebrations focused on dancing. Social dances ("intertribals") are mixed with traditional competition dances.

Group of Ojibwa children at a powwow

GETTING AN EDUCATION
Since the 1960s Canadian and U.S. governments have provided funds for new education programs run by the tribes themselves. New schools (teaching in both the tribal language and English) mean that nearly all reservation children now attend school.

NORTHWEST TERRITORIES TRIBAL MEETING
In the 1970s new legal help groups, such as the Native American Rights Fund, won cases before the U.S. Indian Claims Commission. Set up in 1946, it settles land claims arising from broken treaties. The Lakota have received $105 million, and tribes in Maine were awarded $40 million. The Canadian government and the Inuit agreed on a new self-governing Inuit territory (Nunavut) in 1991.

Did you know?

FASCINATING FACTS

▲ North American Indian tribes have an important influence on the world's cuisines. Experts say that an incredible 60 per cent of the food eaten across the globe today—from tomatoes and potatoes to peppers and peanuts—is derived from plants originally domesticated by Native Americans.

Eagle-feather trim

▲ The buffalo provided food, clothing, and shelter to Great Plains natives. No part of this beast went to waste. Its hooves were made into rattles; dice and toys were carved from its bones; the brains were used to tan hides; its dung was burned as fuel; and the bladder became a storage bag. Even the skin from its tough neck did double duty as a shield.

▲ The Pueblo people didn't need an alarm system to keep intruders away. Instead, they built the entrances to their living areas (and valuable food stores) in the pueblo roof. The ladders that helped them reach these entrances could be pulled away before an enemy could scramble up them to get to the goods.

Tough surface to deflect arrows

Buffalo-neck shield

▲ It's not at all chilly inside an igloo. The long entrance tunnels keep out icy winds, and in the domed main area, whale blubber burns in simple stone lamps to raise the temperature inside to about the same as your heated living room.

▲ In the winter, Cherokee tribespeople enjoyed a rowdy celebration called the Booger Dance. After all the guests had arrived, four masked dancers called boogers would run into the house, chasing women and making loud noises.

Sheets of bark were laid over a wood frame

▲ Northwestern tribes carved fantastic animal designs into their houses and tall totem poles. Many carvings depicted all sides of an animal—even its insides! The carvings were painted with dyes made from vegetables. Red, black, and white were the most commonly used colors.

▲ Tribespeople developed a strong working knowledge of herbal medicines. For example, they treated minor aches with a substance from willow bark that was later found to be salicylic acid, an ingredient in aspirin.

▲ A favorite snack among natives of central California was roasted grasshopper.

▲ From snowshoes to storage boxes, tribes of the Northeastern woodlands used trees as raw material for building houses as well as hundreds of household essentials. Tree roots could be rolled to make string, while tree burls could be made into food bowls or cooking pots. Lightweight canoes made from birch bark sheets were waterproofed with a thick coat of spruce resin.

▲ Almost every Navajo family kept sheep, using the woolly fleece to weave warm blankets. Some Navajo parents believed that rubbing spiderwebs into their infant daughters' palms would help them develop good weaving skills.

Totem pole

▲ The Coast Salish tribe bred small, woolly dogs. In springtime, they sheared them, spun the dog hair into yarn, and wove warm fabric from the yarn.

▲ Iroquois women owned the harvest because they planted and tended crops. If a woman was angry with her husband, she had the right to refuse him any of her food.

▲ Tattoos were popular among many Southwestern tribes. These were made by pricking the skin with a cactus needle and rubbing charcoal into the marks.

▲ Californian tribes were expert basket weavers. The Pomo tribe is famous for its intricate, feather-trimmed basketry that ranged from thimble-sized to three feet tall. Weavers even made tiny baskets the size of a pinhead to show off their skills.

Beads and feathers decorate this basket

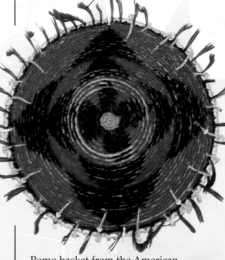

Pomo basket from the American Museum of Natural History

Birchbark canoe

Q What is the difference between North American Indians, Native Americans, First Nations people, and indigenous people?

A The first three are synonyms. They all refer to the same people. But "indigenous people" refers to any culture that lived in a place first. So North American Indians are all indigenous people, but not all indigenous people are North American Indians; Africa, for example, has its own indigenous people.

Small feathers attached to the ends

Large eagle feathers sway as the dancer waves the wand

Cherokee dance wand

Q Which name is the right one to use?

Dance club

A Although some people have a preference for one name over another, none are considered offensive. Most North American Indians in the United States prefer to identify themselves by tribe, however. Most people in Canada use "First Nations."

Q How many North American Indians are there today, and where do they live?

A According to the latest U.S. Census, there are about two million North American Indians living in the United States and one million in Canada. About half of all Native Americans live west of the Mississippi River. One in five Native Americans lives on a reservation.

Q Is there a single Native American religion?

A No, there is no single religion, but most North American Indian belief systems share a strong link with the spirit world and its power over people's lives.

Q What is a tribe, and how many are there?

A A tribe is a group of North American Indians with the same language, customs, and religious beliefs. There are at least 300 different tribes.

Ute good luck lizard

Q What is the spirit world? What is its power?

A The belief that invisible forces or spirits affect life in the visible world is sacred in Native American religions. Shamans are in touch with this spirit world, and can use its power to heal people, protect a tribe, or ensure a good hunt or harvest. Many tribes "see" spirit power in the things that are important to their survival. For example, there are rain spirits in the desert and buffalo spirits on the Great Plains.

Q Are there Native American holidays?

A There are plenty of celebrations among the different tribes. Some ceremonies happen once a year while others are seasonal. There are harvest festivals, dances to celebrate peace or call people to war, coming-of-age rituals, and ceremonies created to bring good luck to the tribe.

Q How many Native Americans languages are there?

A Before European contact with the tribes that lived in North America (c.1500), an estimated 500 or more languages were spoken. We don't know how many languages there are, because not everyone agrees on which languages are unique. If two languages are similar enough that speakers can usually undestand each other, they are considered dialects of the same language.

Q How do Native Americans believe the world was created?

A Some tribes tell of a single Creator, while others believe that life was born from Mother Earth. Many tribes believe life sprung from water, as spirits collected mud to make the Earth. Others tell of humans climbing through underground worlds to Earth's surface. Another common theme is an animal or spiritual assistant who helps humans.

Record Breakers

TALLEST TOTEM POLE

A In 1994, a gigantic totem pole known as the Spirit of Lekwammen was raised in Victoria, British Columbia. It was just over 180 feet (54 m) tall; in 1997, it was shortened due to safety concerns.

OLDEST AND LONGEST SURVIVING MOUND

A The Serpent Mound in Adena, OH is a 1,330-foot- (405-m-) long effigy mound in the form of a giant serpent. It was built by the Adena peoples in the first century C.E.

OLDEST CONTINUALLY INHABITED VILLAGE IN AMERICA

A The Acoma Pueblo in New Mexico has been inhabited since about 1150 C.E. This village, known as the Sky City, is build on a tall sandstone mesa.

Who's who?

NATIVE AMERICAN HISTORY IS THE STORY of its people; here are the stories behind some of the people who helped shape and create that history. From prophets to potters, from warriors on the battlefield to fighters for peace, here is a glimpse into the lives and achievements of many well-known Native American tribespeople.

BLACK ELK

Lakota Black Elk (1863–1950) had a vision as a child that led to his training as a holy man. When U.S. government agents began to outlaw some of the Lakota's religious ceremonies, Black Elk acted to preserve the culture of his people. He told his story to poet John C. Neihardt, who captured the Lakota way of life in his 1932 book, *Black Elk Speaks.*

Breastplate rods made from bone or buffalo horn

Red Cloud, Lakota chief

BLACK HAWK

Chief of a Sac tribe, Black Hawk (1767–1837) did not approve when a small group of tribe members sold 15 million acres of land to the government. When forced to leave their ancestral home, Black Hawk led other members of his tribe in a fierce resistance. They were eventually vanquished at the Battle of Bad Axe.

CRAZY HORSE

In his early teens, Crazy Horse was making a name for himself as a brave warrior. By the time he was 20, this Lakota leader had already led his first war party. Crazy Horse (1849–1877) became a legend not only for his daring and skill on the battlefield, but for his dedication to preserving the traditional way of life of his people. With Sitting Bull, Crazy Horse helped lead tribespeople to victory at the Battle of Little Bighorn.

ADA DEER

Born in 1935, Ada Deer grew up on a Menominee reservation. In 1970, the government decided to dissolve the reservation. Deer fought back, traveling to Washington, D.C. to tell Congress the government was breaking its promise. The government admitted its mistake. Later, Deer was named assistant secretary of the Bureau of Indian Affairs, the first Native American woman to hold that post.

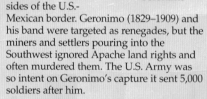

GERONIMO

This Apache warrior and his band were notorious on both sides of the U.S.-Mexican border. Geronimo (1829–1909) and his band were targeted as renegades, but the miners and settlers pouring into the Southwest ignored Apache land rights and often murdered them. The U.S. Army was so intent on Geronimo's capture it sent 5,000 soldiers after him.

Geronimo

IRA HAYES

During World War II, Pima tribemember Ira Hayes (1923–1955) was one of the six U.S. Marines who raised an American flag at Iwo Jima. Even though the island was under intense gunfire, Hayes and his fellow Marines showed bravery. A photographer captured the scene, and a famous sculpture is based on his photograph.

HIAWATHA

Iroquois leader Hiawatha (c. 1550s) was a member of the Onondaga tribe. His wife and children were murdered, but instead of seeking revenge, he traveled among the Iroquois tribes spreading a message that all people should live in peace.

CHIEF JOSEPH

One of the very last Native Americans to surrender to U.S. government forces, Nez Perce leader Chief Joseph (1840–1904) fought tooth and nail against the forced removal of his people. His band outfought—and outfoxed—the army for four months until, weary of war and worried about his people, he finally surrendered.

Crazy Horse Memorial, South Dakota

LITTLE CROW

Dakota Sioux leader Little Crow (c. 1810–1863) made a treaty with the United States to give up land for financial aid, but it was broken. Without the food and supplies they were promised, the tribe faced starvation. They waged all-out war but the army prevailed; 38 tribespeople were hanged in 1862, the largest mass execution in U.S. history.

MARIA MARTINEZ

As a girl, Pueblo Maria Martinez (c. 1887–1980) learned from her elders how to make clay pottery. Pueblo pots were usually fired on a bed of hot coals to harden them. Martinez experimented by burning dung on the coals, creating a cloud of smoke to darken the pot to a rich black. Designs painted on the pot beforehand appeared in a glossy black sheen. Her pottery became famous throughout the world.

Chief Joseph of the Nez Perce tribe

MASSASOIT

The chief of the Wampanoag people, Massasoit (c. 1590–1661) lived in present-day Massachussetts. He was among the North American Indians who joined the Pilgrims at Plymouth for a feast of thanksgiving after the successful harvest of 1621. Massasoit and his tribespeople had helped the new arrivals learn how to farm the land and maintained generally peaceful relations with the Pilgrims.

METACOM

In 1675, groups of Wampanoag and Narragansett Indians led by Metacom (1640–1676) waged war with settlers on the Plymouth Colony. Though Metacom, nicknamed "King Phillip" by the English after an ancient king, was a skilled warrior, his band was soon overpowered, but not before 600 English settlers and 3,000 tribespeople had been killed.

CYNTHIA PARKER

As a young pioneer girl, nine-year-old Cynthia Parker (1827–1870) was taken captive by a party of Commanche warriors. She was eventually adopted by the tribe and given a new name. Parker loved the people and married a tribe warrior. But when her husband was away, she was recaptured and sent back to her family.

POCAHONTAS

The daughter of a powerful Powhatan leader in what is now Virginia, Pocahontas (c. 1517–1596) was about 11 years old when English colonists arrived at Jamestown. Her tribe had a friendly relationship with the colonists, but in the midst of tricky negotiations, colonists kidnapped Pocahontas and used her as a bargaining tool. She later married a colonist and was the toast of London on a visit to England, but nobody really knows how much say she had in these decisions.

RED CLOUD

This Lakota war chief and his band attacked U.S. forts in present-day Montana and Colorado time and time again until the army eventually gave up. Red Cloud (1822–1909) was equally renowned as a statesman. The government eventually negotiated a peace treaty with Red Cloud, bringing a temporary peace to the Plains.

Pocahontas

SACAJAWEA

When Merriwether Lewis and William Clark set out on Thomas Jefferson's orders to explore the newly acquired western territories of the United States, the pair enlisted a Shoshone woman named Sacajawea (c. 1790–c. 1812) as a guide and interpreter. Her skills were invaluable to the expedition; when other tribespeople saw her, they knew the party was on a peaceful mission because no war party would include a woman.

Sacajawea dollar

SEQUOYAH

This Cherokee man worked alone for many years to invent a way of writing down his native language. Sequoyah (c. 1770–1843) used symbols to represent each sound in the Cherokee language. Almost overnight, his people became literate; in 1828, Cherokees began publishing their own newspaper with Sequoyah's writing system.

SITTING BULL

A respected leader and a brave warrior, Lakota Sioux chief Sitting Bull (c. 1831–1890) led his people during their war with U.S. forces. He led the Lakota to victory at the Battle of Little Bighorn. In his later years he continued to serve as a leader, urging his people to keep their own ways alive.

SQUANTO

Imagine how surprised the Pilgrims must have been when, in 1621, Squanto (c. ?–1622) walked into their settlement and greeted them—in English. Little about this Patuxet native's early life is known, but he was kidnapped by English explorers surveying the area and taken to England, where he learned the language. After returning to the colonies, he helped the Pilgrims plant crops and communicate with the local tribes.

TECUMSEH

After the Revolutionary War, settlers pushed into the Ohio River Valley, driving tribes from their lands. Shawnee leader Tecumseh (c. 1768–1813) was determined that the only way Native Americans could be heard was to speak in one voice. He traveled through present-day Ohio, Michigan, Indiana, and Illinois persuading tribes to join his confederation, but was killed in battle before his dreams were realized.

TENSKWATAWA (THE PROPHET)

Tecumseh's brother, Tenskwatawa (c. 1775–c. 1837), was a religious leader who traveled tribal territories with one message: tribes must avoid contact with white people. Known as The Prophet, he also urged tribes to work to preserve their native cultures and customs.

SARAH WINNEMUCCA

A Paiute native who also mastered English, Spanish, and three other native languages, Sarah Winnemucca (c. 1844–1891) worked as an interpreter and negotiator during the Paiute Wars. After the fighting was over, she wrote books and gave speeches critical of the whites who handled Native American affairs. Her work was an important early example of the expanding Native American rights movement.

Buckskin dress trimmed with beads and fringe

Sarah Winnemucca

ZINTKALA NUNI

Four days after the massacre at Wounded Knee in 1890, people arriving to search for survivors were startled by the cries of a tiny baby. She was wearing a cap decorated with red, white, and blue beadwork in the shape of the American flag. The girl (c. 1890–1919) was named Zintkala Nuni, or Lost Bird, and adopted by an army brigadier general. She was raised as a white girl but grew unhappy; as an adult she returned to the Sioux but they rejected her. Her story inspired the foundation of the Lost Bird society, a group that offers support to Indians adopted by non-Native parents.

Tribes by region

- **NORTHEAST** Algonquian, Huron, Iroquois, Micmac, Pequot, Shawnee, Wampanoag

- **SOUTHEAST** Cherokee, Chickasaw, Choctaw, Creek, Timucua, Yuchi

- **GREAT PLAINS** Blackfeet, Cheyenne, Comanche, Crow, Osage, Pawnee, Quapaw, Sioux

- **PLATEAU AND GREAT BASIN** Bannock, Cayuse, Kootenai, Nez Perce, Paiute, Shoshone, Spokane, Umatilla, Ute, Yakima

- **SOUTHWEST** Apache, Havasupai, Navajo, Pima, Pueblos

- **CALIFORNIA** Cahuilla, Chumash, Hupa, Maidu, Miwok, Pomo, Yurok

- **NORTHWEST COAST** Chinook, Haida, Kwakiutl, Makah, Nootka, Tlingit, Tsimshian

- **ARCTIC** Inuit, Aleut

- **SUBARCTIC** Carrier, Cree, Chippewyan, Kutchin, Montagnais, Naskapi

Find out more

BEAUTIFUL BASKETRY
If you visit a museum, look closely at the artistry of objects in the collection. This basket, for example, was designed for ordinary, everyday use, but it is still extraordinary to look at.

This basket from the California area is woven so tightly it can hold water

NATURAL BEAUTY
For hundreds of years, North American Indians had to make or trade for everything they needed to survive. Many of these objects are now on display in museums. You'll see how the natural beauty that surrounded the tribespeople—feathers, wood, sand, shells, clay, and plants—was turned into beautiful man-made objects.

Paintings record local history and legend

To GET THE INSIDE STORY of the tribes and their traditions, you might want to start by researching the tribes that originally inhabited the place where you live. Many local museums and historical societies house small North American Indian collections. Museums in the nation's capital and other large cities typically contain larger collections relating to our country's first inhabitants, from everyday objects to special ceremonial artifacts. You can also visit "living" museums and reservations that allow you to really step inside the daily lives of the first Americans. Or, check the Internet or your newspaper for local Native American cultural events.

MUSEUM OF AMERICAN INDIAN
Part of the Smithsonian Institution, the National Museum of the American Indian contains an amazing collection of important artifacts from every culture area in the United States. The museum curators have taken care to ensure that all objects in the collection have been obtained fairly through purchase or donation.

Ears of maize hung in rows to dry

USEFUL WEB SITES

- A portal site for a huge range of Native American resources on the Web:
  www.nativeculture.com
- Home page of the National Congress of American Indians:
  www.naci.org
- Take a virtual tour through the National Museum of the American Indian:
  www.nmai.si.edu
- A daily on-line newspaper for the Native American community:
  www.indiancountry.com
- The Library of Congress collection of more than 7 million digital items relating to the culture and history of the United States; has a strong Native American section:
  http://memory.loc.gov
- An introduction to the histories of 48 Native American tribes:
  www.tolatsga.org/Compacts.html
- Interesting articles about Native American art and technology:
  www.nativetech.org
- Home page of the National Congress of American Indians:
  www.naci.org

WEAVER
While you can admire Native American art in a museum, it is even more impressive to see it being made. This Navajo woman is weaving a blanket on a loom, in a traditional tribal design. You can also see potters, basketweavers, beadworkers, quillers, and wood and ivory carvers at work, keeping native art traditions alive.

Geometric patterns are a tribal tradition

Places to Visit

AMERICAN MUSEUM OF NATURAL HISTORY, NEW YORK, NY
Explore the museum's Culture Halls to see Native American artifacts, art, and folklore. The Hall of Northwest Coast Indians is the museum's oldest.

THE FIELD MUSEUM, CHICAGO, IL
Visit the amazing permanent collections and explore a full-scale Pawnee earth lodge exhibit.

NATIONAL MUSEUM OF THE AMERICAN INDIAN, WASHINGTON, D.C.
This museum, opened in 2004, contains thousands of objects of cultural and historical interest; its spiritual objects are on display with permission of the relevant tribe.

SOUTHWEST MUSEUM OF THE AMERICAN INDIAN, LOS ANGELES, CA
This museum houses one of the most important collections of Native American artifacts in the United States.

CRAZY HORSE MEMORIAL FOUNDATION CRAZY HORSE, SD
See the world's largest sculpture in progress, and visit the excellent museum and cultural center. Check the Internet for special events.

HEARD MUSEUM, PHOENIX, AZ
For more than 75 years this museum has collected the finest examples of Native American artifacts with a particular emphasis on tribes from the Southwest.

CHEROKEE NATIONAL MUSEUM, TAHLEQUAH, OK
This museum features two living history sites: a village recreating the time before European contact and a town representing the later days of the tribe.

DANCES WITH WOLVES
In film and television, the story of Native Americans has not always been told with accuracy. But actor/director Kevin Costner's 1990 movie *Dances With Wolves* was a step in the right direction. Its characters and their cause were treated with sympathy. The Native American actors spoke in their own Sioux language, another breakthrough.

Traditional feathered headdress

PUEBLO KITCHEN
Would you like to step into the past? Many "living history" sites around the country feature historically accurate recreations of Native American dwellings. The layout, food storage methods, and utensils in this pueblo kitchen are so realistic, you can almost smell the corncakes frying! State tourism boards and the Internet will help you to find living history museums to visit.

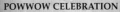

POWWOW CELEBRATION
While many museums focus on how tribes used to live before contact with Europeans, it is important to remember that Native Americans are still a vital part of our culture today. The best way to see this for yourself is to attend a cultural celebration like a powwow. From rodeos to art fairs, you'll see how modern tribes are keeping their ancient traditions alive. Check the Internet to find an event.

Glossary

ABALONE A marine animal with an oval, nearly spiral shell

ADOBE Clay bricks hardened in the Sun; used by some tribes in the Southwestern culture area to construct buildings

ARTISAN A highly skilled worker or craftsperson

BABICHE Thongs or laces made of rawhide, eel skins, or animal sinew; used for tying or weaving

BREECHCLOTH A cloth worn around the loins; also known as a loincloth

BUCKSKIN A type of soft yet durable leather made from the skin of a deer

BULLBOAT A one-person craft made of a buffalo hide stretched over a frame built from willow tree branches

BUNCH A plume made of quills, feathers, wood, and string worn on the crown of the head in Maidu dances

BURL A knot in the wood of a tree

CALUMET A long-stemmed pipe smoked by Native Americans as a token of peace

CEDE To give up or transfer one's property or rights

CHICKEE A Seminole house built on sticks with open sides and a deeply thatched roof

CHIEF The leader or head of a tribe, respected for his wisdom and experience. A tribe might have one or many chiefs

CHOKECHERRIES The bitter fruits of a wild North American cherry tree

CHUNKEY A stick-throwing game very popular among tribes of the Southeastern area

CLAN Any group of people with a common ancestor

CONFEDERATION The name for a political alliance between two or more tribes

COPPER A shield-shaped plaque of engraved metal used as a symbol of wealth in the Northwestern area.

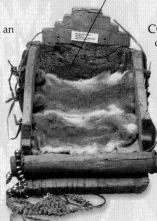

Fur-lined carrier keeps babies snug and warm

Cradleboard

COUNCIL A group of representatives chosen to make decisions; a Great Council had representatives from several tribes to make collective decisions.

CRADLEBOARD A rigid baby carrier made of thick twigs covered in soft animal skin; could be carried on the back, attached to a horse, or propped up

CULTURE The set of customs and beliefs that shape a group of people's way of life

CUPOLA A small dome-shaped structure on a roof

DUGOUT A canoe made by setting a log on fire, then digging out its charred insides

ELDER An older person with the respect of, or authority over, a tribe

FLAIL An agricultural tool made of a swinging stick tied to the end of a long handle; used to thresh grain by hand

GANS Apache mountain spirit beings wearing masks, headdresses, and body paint; the Gans dance is part of both healing and coming-of-age rituals

GORGET A decorative plate hung around the neck to rest on the chest

GRAVE BOX The name for the coffin-like box of the Northwestern area.

GRAVE HOUSE A house, sometimes as large as a regular house, built to hold the grave box

IGLOO A dome-shaped Inuit house made of blocks of ice

KACHINA In Pueblo folklore, a helpful spirit represented by a doll or costumed dancer

KACHINA DOLLS Carved dolls representing the different types of kachina; used to teach children about the spirits and their roles

Kachina doll

KAYAK A lightweight, one-person canoe made of animal skins stretched across a wooden frame

KIVA An underground chamber where Pueblo people held sacred ceremonies

LACROSSE A Native American stick-and-ball game in which two teams of players try to advance a small ball across the field and into the opposing team's goal

LODGE Tribal housing; may also be the collective name for all who live together inside it

LONGHOUSE A barn-shaped, multi-family dwelling made from a sapling frame covered in bark shingles; typical of the Iroquois

LYE A strong alkaline solution; sometimes obtained by leaching wood ashes

MAIZE Another name for corn

MIGRATION The movement of a people from one place to another

MISSION A religious center where missionaries try to convert native peoples to their religion

MOCCASINS A shoe made of soft, whipstiched leather

NOMADIC Of a group of people who have no permanent home, but instead move about constantly in search of food

PALISADE A fence made from a row of large pointed stakes sunk in the ground

PARFLECHE A folding rawhide case, large enough to carry food or clothing.

PEMMICAN An energy-rich, long-lasting, and easy-to-carry food made by pounding dried meat, fat, and berries together; similar to beef jerky

Potlatch dress

POTLATCH An important ceremony among tribes in the Northwestern culture area in which the host gives lavish gifts and food to his or her guests

POWWOW A festival where tribes gather to sing, dance, and celebrate their shared heritage

PRAIRIE A large area of level or slightly rolling grasslands

PUEBLO The clay-walled, multi-family dwellings built by the Pueblo people

QUILLWORK The art of decorating clothing and objects with porcupine quill embroidery

Pueblos were built of sandstone plastered with mud or adobe bricks.

QUIRT A type of riding whip with a braided lash and a short, stubby handle

RAWHIDE Tough animal skins that have not been tanned to soften them

REMOVAL The policy of the U.S. government to force tribes to leave their homelands and settle elsewhere

RESERVATION An area of land set aside by the government for the sole use of an officially recognized tribe

ROACH A headdress made from dyed animal hair worn by warriors in raiding parties in the Great Lakes region

SHAMAN A religious leader who used medicines to heal the sick

Roach

Dakota shaman's bag

SINEW An animal tendon

SOUL CATCHER A shaman's instrument; used to capture a sick person's soul and return it to his body

SPIRIT WORLD The invisible but invincible power that fills the world in Native North American belief; shamans capture and direct some of this spirit to manipulate the ordinary world

SWEAT LODGE A dome-shaped structure of bent sticks covered in animal hides and heated by steam; people went inside to cleanse themselves before religious ceremonies.

TEPEE A tall, cone-shaped house made of animal skins over a framework of poles; typical among the Plains people

TOTEM POLE A towering sculpture made by members of the Northwestern tribes by carving animals, humans, and spirit faces into logs

TRAVOIS A carrying device made by suspending a wooden platform on two poles, dragged along by a horse or dogs

TREATY A written agreement between two nations

TRIBE A group of people with common language, customs, and religious beliefs; tribes live together under one or more leaders called chiefs.

UMIAK A large, open boat made of animal skins stretched over a wooden frame

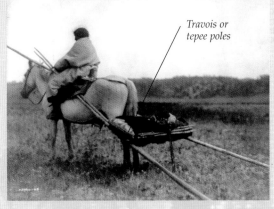

Travois or tepee poles

Great Plains natives used the travois to move teepees, household goods, and food.

WAMPUM Small seashells used to keep tribal records and as a form of currency; usually fashioned into strings or belts; dark purple or black beads were the most valuable.

WARP In weaving, the threads running lengthwise on the loom

WEFT In weaving, the threads carried by the shuttle back and forth across the warp

WEIR A low dam or obstruction built in a river to back up or redirect the water

WIGWAM A cone-shaped house made of saplings covered with grass or bark mats

WIKIUP An oval-shaped, portable shelter made of sticks and dried grass

YUCCA The white-flowered plant of the agave family with stiff, sword-shaped leaves; woven by California tribes into clothing and household objects

Index

Acknowledgments

The publisher would like to thank:
The American Museum of Natural History, especially Anibal Rodriguez and Judith Levinson (Anthropology); John Davey (Publications); Deborah Barral, Mark Gostnell, Lize Mogel, Alan Walker, Marco Hernandez, and Rob Muller (Exhibitions); Joe Donato, Tony Macaluso, Martin Daly, Eadwinn Brookes, and Aldwin Phillip (Electricians); Eddy Garcia (Maintenance). Leslie Gerhauser, photographic assistance. Sally Rose, additional research. Helena Spiteri, Tim Button, Sophy D'Angelo,
Ivan Finnegan, Kati Poynor, and Susan St. Louis for editorial and design assistance.
Dave King and Kate Warren for extra photography, Museum of Mankind.
Artwork: John Woodcock
Picture credits
(t=top b=bottom c=center l=left r=right a=above)
American Indian Contemporary Art: Larry McNeil, 62bl. American Museum of Natural History: 36tl (no. 335493), 43cb (no. 2A342), 52cbr (no. 44309), 56cbr (no. 121545); E.S. Curtis 39tr (no. 335534), 46tl (no. 335553A); J.K. Dixon 28b (no.

316642). Bridgeman Art Library: D.F. Barry, Bismarck, Dakota 31c; British Museum 18c; Private Collection 32c; Royal Ontario Museum, Toronto 59cbr. Trustees of The British Museum: 9cl, 9c. Colorific!/Black Star: J. Cammick 63cl; P.S. Mecca 62r. Service de la Marine 45cb. Hutchison Libary: Moser 63br. The Image Bank: Marvin Newman 40tl. Ann Ronan Image Select: 16tr. Collections of the Library of Congress: 30cr. Magnum Photos: E. Arnold 31tr. Mansell Collection: 25cbr, 25b, 49cr. Minnesota Historical Society: 33c. Montana Historical Society, Helena: 34tr. Nevada Historical Society, Reno: 40cra, 41tr. Peter Newark's Western Americana: jacket, 10ca, 10cb, 12ca, 14tl, 19tr, 21br, 23tl, 27cr, 28c, 33tl, 34c, 37bl, 40tl, 46clb. The Arizona Historical Society, Tucson 48tr. Rochester Museum and Science Center, Rochester, NY: (*Formation of the League*, Ernest Smith) 14cr. Royal Ontario Museum, Toronto: (detail from *Hunting Moose Deer in Winter*) 59tr. Service de la Marine, Vincennes: (detail from *Culture & Stationis Ratio*, de Bry) 17br. Smithsonian Institution: Department of Anthropology 30/31 (cat. no. 358425); National Anthropological Archives 19br, 26bc, 27tcr, 30tr, 35tr, 41tl, 42cra, 50cra, 60bcr. Courtesy of The Southwest Museum, Los Angeles: 22c. Frank Spooner

Pictures/Gamma: A. Ribeiro 63cr. Trip/Eye Ubiquitous: L Fordyce 63bc. Every effort has been made to trace the copyright holders of photographs. The publishers apologize for any omissions and will amend further editions.

Corbis: Bettmann 67bl; Christie's Images 68tl; CORBIS SYGMA 69c; Kevin R. Morris 69br; Pete Saloutos 69tl. Crazy Horse Memorial Archives: Robb DeWall 66tr, 68bl. Dorling Kindersley: 64tr; Alan Keohane, Courtesy of the Hopi Learning Centre, Arizona 70bl; Andrew Leyerle 67tr; Francesca Yorke 68br, 70tl, 71tr; Lynton Gardiner, Courtesy of The American Museum of Natural History 64tl, 64br, 65bl, 65tl, 65tr, 70br, 71cl, 71bl. The Granger Collection: 66l, 66br, 67br. Library of Congress Prints and Photographs Division: 66c, 71cr.
National Museum of the American Indian: Robert C. Lautman 68cr.

Front cover:
Tcl: Lynton Gardiner © Dorling Kindersley, Courtesy of The American Museum of Natural History; Tc: © American Museum of Natural History; Tr: Lynton Gardiner © Dorling Kindersley, Courtesy of The American Museum of Natural History; B: © CORBIS.

Back cover: C & br: Lynton Gardiner © Dorling Kindersley, Courtesy of The American Museum of Natural History.